D0756575

THE LITTLE BOOK OF
RUGBY
FACTS

EDDIE RYAN

MERCIER PRESS
Irish Publisher – Irish Story

MERCIER PRESS

Cork

www.mercierpress.ie

© Eddie Ryan, 2015

ISBN: 978 1 78117 327 5

10 9 8 7 6 5 4 3 2 1

A CIP record for this title is available from the British Library.

Printed and bound in the EU.

CONTENTS

THE BRITISH AND IRISH LIONS

– The British and Irish Lions first came into existence in 1888 as the Shaw & Shrewsbury Team. It mainly comprised English players, but also contained players from Scotland and Wales. The team would later be known as the British Isles team.

– Their first tour was not sanctioned by rugby authorities and was sponsored by businessmen Arthur Shrewsbury and Alfred Shaw, after whom the team was named.

– The Lions played no Test matches on their first tour. The games were against provincial, academic and club sides only.

– The nickname 'the Lions' was first used by British and South African journalists on the 1924 South African tour, after the lion emblem on the team's ties. The lion had earlier been used as the emblem on their jerseys, but was replaced by the four-sectioned badge containing the crests of the four represented unions in 1924.

– On the 1950 tour of New Zealand and Australia, the name British Lions was officially adopted.

– William and Edward Bromet were the first pair of brothers to be capped together in a Lions Test match. The English duo featured together in two internationals on the 1891 tour of South Africa.

– The 1888 tourists played sixteen games in Australia and a further nineteen in New Zealand. But they didn't just play rugby union against their hosts. They also took part in nineteen Australian Rules football matches, which helped fund the tour.

– In 1936 the Lions visited Argentina for a second tour (the first had been in 1927). They won all ten of their matches and conceded only 12 points in the whole tour.

– Lewis Jones is the only Lion to have scored a full house in a Test match on tour. He was a late replacement when the Lions travelled to Australia and New Zealand in 1950. The Welsh teenager was in dominant form, scoring two conversions, two penalties, a drop goal and a try in the first Test win over the Wallabies.

– Willie John McBride of Ireland holds the all-time appearance record. The Irish second row wore the Lions jersey on seventy occasions across five tours in 1962, 1966, 1968, 1971 and 1974. Fellow Irish warrior Mike Gibson is a close second with sixty-eight appearances.

– The record for the highest number of points scored by a Lion in a single fixture is held by Alan Old. The England fly-half scored an impressive

37 points in the 97–0 win over South West Districts on the 1974 tour of South Africa. His haul of points included a try, a penalty and fifteen conversions.

– Since the 2001 tour of Australia, the official name British and Irish Lions has been used. The team is still often referred to simply as the Lions.

– Paul O'Connell's appointment as captain for the 2009 tour saw the Lions follow a familiar pattern. The Irish lock's selection meant that the two most recent (at the time) Lions tours had been led by Irishmen, with the two previous tours skippered by an Englishman, and the two before that by Scotsmen.

– Team coaches are a relatively new phenomenon for the tourists. The Lions didn't travel with a coach until the 1966 tour, when John Robins took on the role, although he was officially described as an assistant manager.

– The Lions' second-Test win over Australia in Sydney in 1950 was a big scalp for the visitors. The support for the natives appeared to be elsewhere. A crowd of 25,000 turned up for the final Test. This was some 50,000 fewer than were in attendance at a local rugby league match, played at the adjacent Sydney Oval.

– In 1989 the Lions played a Test series in Australia for the first time since 1966. It was certainly worth the wait. After losing the first Test by 18 points, they battled back to win the Battle of Ballymore in game two. Sir Ian McGeechan's squad put the seal on a series win in Sydney. A try by Ieuan Evans and five penalties from Gavin Hastings were enough to land the spoils.

– Paul O'Connell may have been the tenth Irishman to captain the Lions but he was just the second Munster player to do so. O'Connell led the Lions in South Africa in 2009, forty-one years after full-back Tom Kiernan did the same.

– Representing your country as captain is no guarantee of making the Lions selection. The captains of England, Scotland and Wales all missed out on initial selection for the 2009 Lions tour. Steve Borthwick, Mike Blair and Ryan Jones didn't make Sir Ian McGeechan's original squad for the trip to South Africa, despite being their countries' captains at the time of selection.

– The youngest Lion on that 2009 tour to South Africa was Leigh Halfpenny, aged just twenty. The oldest player was England's Simon Shaw, who was approaching thirty-six by the time the Lions left for home.

– The 2013 British and Irish Lions players had eighty-three different items of playing kit for their tour of Australia and Hong Kong, as well as three Thomas Pink team outfits!

- The record number of points scored in New Zealand and Australia is 842 (by the 1959 Lions, across thirty-three games).

- Martin Johnson of England became the first player to captain two Lions tours, when he led the tourists to Australia in 2001.

- As well as rugby, Lions centre Jack Matthews was well versed in the Marquess of Queensberry Rules. He boxed against the legendary Rocky Marciano. Matthews, who was a Lion in 1950 and also a tour doctor in 1980, drew his contest with the unbeaten future heavyweight world champion at RAF St Athan in 1943.

- As the Lions represent two nation states, they do not have a national anthem. For the 2005 tour to New Zealand the Lions management commissioned a song. 'The Power of Four' never caught the imagination of supporters, however, and was not used on the 2009 or 2013 tours.

- The Lions played an unofficial international match in 1955 at Cardiff Arms Park against a Welsh XV as part of the seventy-fifth anniversary of the Welsh Rugby Union. While the Lions won 20–17, the team did not include most of the big names of the 1955 tour, such as Tony O'Reilly, Jeff Butterfield, Phil Davies, Dickie Jeeps, Bryn Meredith and Jim Greenwood.

- 1977 was a historic year for the Lions as they

played their first official home game, against the Barbarians. The charity fund-raiser was held as part of the Queen's silver jubilee celebrations. The Baa-Baas line-up featured a host of rugby greats, including J. P. R. Williams, Gerald Davies, Gareth Edwards, Jean-Pierre Rives and Jean-Claude Skrela. The Lions included the majority of the team that had played in the fourth Test against New Zealand three weeks before, and won 23–14.

– In 1986 a match was organised against a Rest of the World XV as a warm-up to that year's South Africa tour. Although the tour was subsequently cancelled, the match marked the centenary of the International Rugby Football Board (it later became the International Rugby Board). The Rest of the World XV won 15–7.

– The Lions, led by Rob Andrew, were triumphant against France in Paris in 1989. The game was part of the bicentennial celebrations of the French Revolution. The Lions won 29–27.

– In 1990 a squad called the Four Home Unions played against a Rest of Europe XV. The fixture was used to raise money for the rebuilding of Romania following the overthrow of Nicolae Ceauşescu in December 1989. The team used the Lions logo, as it depicts the crests of the Four Home Unions united in a shield.

- Andy Irvine of Scotland is the all-time points record holder, with 274. Phil Bennett of Wales is next on 228, with England's Bob Hiller a close third on 216 points.

- The Lions have played 618 matches in their history. They have won 457, lost 129 and drawn thirty-two times. The most consecutive wins is twenty-two.

- The most points scored by the Lions in a single match is 116 (against Western Australia in 2001). They also scored the highest number of tries in a Lions match during this game – eighteen.

- The heaviest defeat was against the All Blacks, when the Lions went under by 38 points to 6.

SCORING CHART (includes all 618 fixtures)

Total points for	12,158
Total points against	5,996
Total tries for	2,152
Total tries against	855
Total conversions for	1,156
Total conversions against	399
Total penalty goals for	759
Total penalty goals against	664
Total drop goals for	165
Total drop goals against	91

THE LIONS' TOURING RECORD

Test matches	Played	Won	Lost	Drew
Argentina	7	6	0	1
Australia	23	17	6	0
New Zealand	38	6	29	3
South Africa	46	17	23	6
Total	**114**	**46**	**58**	**10**

THE IRISH PROVINCES

MUNSTER RUGBY

- Munster Rugby was founded in 1879.

- Munster have two main stadiums where they play their home matches: Thomond Park in Limerick and Musgrave Park (renamed Irish Independent Park in 2014) in Cork.

- Thomond Park has a capacity of 25,600, while Musgrave holds 9,500.

- In 1905 Munster played host to the Original All Blacks, the first New Zealand team to tour outside Australasia. The match was played at the Markets Field, Limerick. New Zealand won 33–0.

- Munster played their first-ever match at Thomond Park in 1938, beating Leinster.

- In 1947 Munster were on the verge of the biggest result in their history to that point. Playing Australia at the Mardyke in Cork they were on the cusp of victory when the Australians scored a try in injury time to snatch the win.

- The three crowns on the flag of Munster are thought to represent the three historic kingdoms of Munster: Thomond in the north, Desmond in the south and Ormond in the east.

- A new logo was introduced for the 2003–04 season, when a stag was added to the crowns to represent strength and competitiveness.

- The stag has been associated with Munster folklore as far back as the eleventh century. One of the historic Munster families, the McCarthys, who trace their origins back to the Carthach, the eleventh-century Prince of Munster, had as their coat of arms a red stag on a shield of metal grey.

- The motto of the McCarthy family, *Forti et fideli nihil difficile* (to the brave and the faithful nothing is impossible), has also been adopted by the team.

- Munster was the first Irish provincial side to defeat a major touring team. They defeated Australia 11–8 at Musgrave Park on 25 January 1967.

- On 31 October 1978 Munster became the only Irish side to beat the All Blacks. The 12–0 victory occurred at Thomond Park. Christy Cantillon scored a try, with Munster legend Tony Ward converting. Ward also added a drop goal in each half. The epic win inspired a stage play by John Breen entitled *Alone it Stands*. The victory is also the subject of a book by Alan English called *Stand Up and Fight: When Munster Beat the All Blacks*.

- Munster took part in the Heineken Cup for the first time in 1995. In their first match, captained by Pat Murray, they secured a victory over Swansea at Thomond Park.

– Donncha O'Callaghan, with 263 caps, is the most capped Munster player of all time.

– In 2006 Munster won the all-Irish semi-final of the Heineken Cup, beating Leinster 30–6 at Lansdowne Road. They then defeated French giants Biarritz in the final at the Millennium Stadium in Cardiff.

– Two Munster men have captained the British and Irish Lions: Paul O'Connell and Tom Kiernan.

– Anthony Horgan is the province's top try scorer, with a total of forty-one. He played his last game for Munster on 15 May 2009 in a 36–10 Celtic League win over the Ospreys at Thomond Park. In a fairytale finish to his career, Horgan scored Munster's final try, much to the delight of the home crowd.

Players Who Have Reached 200 Caps for Munster

Anthony Foley (1994–2008): 201 caps

David Wallace (1997–2012): 203 caps

Mick O'Driscoll (1998–2003, 2005–12): 207 caps

Alan Quinlan (1996–2011): 212 caps

John Hayes (1998–2011): 217 caps

Marcus Horan (1999–2013): 225 caps

Peter Stringer (1998–2013): 232 caps

Ronan O'Gara (1997–2013): 240 caps

Donncha O'Callaghan (1998–present): 263 caps

Record Against Touring Sides

1905	New Zealand	Markets Field	0–33	Lost
1947	Australia	Mardyke	5–6	Lost
1951	South Africa	Thomond Park	6–11	Lost
1954	New Zealand	Mardyke	3–6	Lost
1958	Australia	Thomond Park	3–3	Drew
1960	South Africa	Musgrave Park	3–9	Lost
1962	Canada	Musgrave Park	11–8	Won
1963	New Zealand	Thomond Park	3–6	Lost
1967	Australia	Musgrave Park	11–8	Won
1970	South Africa	Thomond Park	9–25	Lost
1973	New Zealand	Musgrave Park	3–3	Drew
1973	Argentina	Thomond Park	12–12	Drew
1974	New Zealand	Thomond Park	4–14	Lost
1976	Australia	Musgrave Park	13–15	Lost
1978	New Zealand	Thomond Park	12–0	Won
1980	Romania	Thomond Park	9–32	Lost
1981	Australia	Musgrave Park	15–6	Won
1984	Australia	Thomond Park	19–31	Lost
1989	New Zealand	Musgrave Park	9–31	Lost
1990	USSR	Clonmel	15–19	Lost

1992	Australia	Musgrave Park	22–19	Won
1996	Samoa	Musgrave Park	25–35	Lost
1996	Australia	Thomond Park	19–55	Lost
1998	Morocco	Thomond Park	49–17	Won
2008	New Zealand	Thomond Park	16–18	Lost
2010	Australia	Thomond Park	15–6	Won

Honours

Heineken Cup/Champions Cup (2): 2006, 2008

Celtic League/Magners League/Pro12 (3): 2003, 2009, 2011 (runners-up: 2006, 2010, 2011, 2012)

Celtic Cup (1): 2005

British and Irish Cup (1): 2012

Irish Interprovincial Championship: 22 wins

Individual Records

Top points scorer: Ronan O'Gara (2,625)

Most appearances: Donncha O'Callaghan (263)

Most tries: Anthony Horgan (41)

British and Irish Lions from Munster

The following Munster players have represented the British and Irish Lions:

W. J. Ashby: 1910; Oliver Piper: 1910; Michael Bradley: 1924; William Roche: 1924; Tom Clifford: 1950; Mick Lane: 1950; Jim McCarthy: 1950; Tom Reid:

1955; Michael English: 1959; Gordon Wood: 1959; Noel Murphy: 1959, 1966; Tom Kiernan: 1962, 1968; Jerry Walsh: 1966; Barry Bresnihan: 1966, 1968; Mick Doyle: 1968; Moss Keane: 1974, 1977; Colm Tucker: 1980; Tony Ward: 1980; Mike Kiernan: 1983; Gerry McLoughlin: 1983; Donal Lenihan: 1983, 1989; Mick Galwey: 1993; Richard Wallace: 1993; Keith Wood: 1997, 2001; Rob Henderson: 2001; Ronan O'Gara: 2001, 2005, 2009; David Wallace: 2001, 2009; John Hayes: 2005, 2009; Donncha O'Callaghan: 2005, 2009; Paul O'Connell: 2005, 2009, 2013; Keith Earls: 2009; Conor Murray: 2013; Simon Zebo: 2013.

LEINSTER RUGBY

- In 1875, in their first ever interprovincial match, Leinster lost to Ulster by a converted try. They went on to beat Munster in their second game by a single penalty goal to nil.

- The Leinster Branch of the IRFU was formed in 1879 at a meeting at 63 Grafton Street to organise the game of rugby football in the province.

- They play their home matches at the RDS Arena (capacity 18,500) and the Aviva Stadium (capacity 51,700). Before this they played their home fixtures at Donnybrook Stadium, which has a capacity of 6,000. When Leinster turned professional, in 1995, the ground was deemed too small to host European matches.

- The first major touring side to play Leinster was a team drawn from the New Zealand Army – the Kiwis – in 1946. The game ended in a 10–10 draw.

- The first official overseas touring side to play Leinster was Australia, in 1957, with the visitors winning 10–8.

- The Leinster Lions name came into existence during the 2001–02 season, as part of a marketing initiative with Leinster's kit sponsors, Canterbury Clothing Company. The name was not retained, although Leo the Lion was retained as the province's mascot.

- Though Leinster now compete in blue, the team wore green during their early years.

- Leinster have sported a harp symbol since their first interprovincial game in 1875. The story of how the harp was adopted as the Leinster symbol comes from the seventeenth century. Apparently Eoghan Ruadh (Owen Roe) Ó Néill, a famous Irish soldier from Ulster, flew a green flag with a golden harp from his ship, the *St Francis*, when it was anchored at Dunkirk. The Leinster connection came when he returned to Ireland in 1642 to help the Irish Confederation, which was headquartered in Kilkenny.

- In 2010 Leinster played a home league game against Munster at the Aviva Stadium, which was the first time the venue sold out.

– In the 2010–11 Heineken Cup Leinster defeated the Leicester Tigers, Saracens and Northampton Saints, as well as French giants Toulouse (who were the defending European champions), Racing Metro and Clermont Auvergne (the French champions).

– In the 2011 Heineken Cup final, at the Millennium Stadium in Cardiff, Leinster were in deep trouble at half-time. Then they scored 27 unanswered points in the second half to win 33–22 and claim their second European crown with the biggest comeback in European cup final history.

– Leinster were chasing a Pro12 and Heineken Cup double in 2011 but lost 19–9 to great rivals Munster in the Pro12 final.

– The following season Leinster hosted Munster, Bath and Cardiff at the Aviva Stadium and remained unbeaten at the ground until December 2012 when they lost 21–28 to ASM Clermont Auvergne.

– On 19 May 2012 Leinster won a record third Heineken Cup in four years with a 42–14 win over Ulster. It was the first final to feature two teams from Ireland.

– Three stars have been added to the Leinster jersey, just above the crest, to represent the three Heineken Cup titles won to date.

- Since turning professional in 1995, Leinster has had eight different coaches, two of whom were Irish. Gerry Murphy acted as interim coach when future Irish international coach Declan Kidney departed in 2005.

- Sean O'Brien and Rob Kearney of Leinster were voted EPCR (European Professional Club Rugby) player of the year in 2011 and 2012 respectively.

- Great rivals Leinster and Munster have played each other eighty-eight times. Leinster have won forty-three times to Munster's forty. There have been only five draws in well over a century of rugby matches.

Honours

Heineken Cup / Champions Cup (3): 2009, 2011, 2012

Amlin European Challenge Cup (1): 2013

Celtic League/Magners League/Pro12 (3): 2002, 2008, 2013 (runners-up: 2006, 2010, 2011, 2012)

British and Irish Cup (1): 2013

Interprovincial Championship: 22 wins

Individual Records

Top points scorer: Felipe Contepomi (1,225)

Most tries: Shane Horgan (69)

Most appearances: Gordon D'Arcy (253)

British and Irish Lions from Leinster

The following Leinster players have represented the British and Irish Lions:

Tom Crean: 1896; Karl Mullen: 1950; Robin Roe: 1955; Tony O'Reilly: 1955, 1959; Niall Brophy: 1959, 1962; Ronnie Dawson: 1959, 1968; Mike Hipwell: 1971; Sean Lynch: 1971; Fergus Slattery: 1971, 1974; Tom Grace: 1974; John Moloney: 1974; Willie Duggan: 1977; Philip Orr: 1977, 1980; Rodney O'Donnell: 1980; John Robbie: 1980; Ollie Campbell: 1980, 1983; Hugo MacNeill: 1983; Paul Dean: 1989; Brendan Mullin: 1989; Vince Cunningham: 1993; Eric Miller: 1997; Malcolm O'Kelly: 2001, 2005; Brian O'Driscoll: 2001, 2005, 2009, 2013; Shane Byrne: 2005; Gordon D'Arcy: 2005, 2009; Denis Hickie: 2005; Shane Horgan: 2005; Rob Kearney: 2009, 2013; Luke Fitzgerald: 2009; Jamie Heaslip: 2009, 2013; Cian Healy: 2013; Sean O'Brien: 2013; Jonathan Sexton: 2013.

CONNACHT RUGBY

–   The Connacht Branch of the IRFU was founded on 8 December 1885.

–   The Galway Sportsground has been the spiritual home of Connacht Rugby since the 1920s. The ground opened in 1927 and has a capacity of 7,500. This can be increased to a maximum of 9,500 when temporary seating is added.

- With just over 7 per cent of the total number of Irish rugby union players, Connacht has the smallest pool of players of the four provinces.

- The IRFU originally designated Connacht as a development team. This meant that they operated on half the budget of the other Irish provincial teams. In 2003 the IRFU proposed shutting down Connacht Rugby as a professional team.

- The Connacht Eagles (formerly known as Connacht A) is the team that represents Connacht in the British and Irish Cup.

- The eagle and the sword arm that form the centre of the Connacht Rugby crest are taken from the flag of the province. The crest was presented to Ruaidrí Ua Conchobair, the King of Connacht, by an Irish monastery founded in Regensburg, Bavaria, in the eleventh century.

- Ciaran Fitzgerald, who has captained the Lions, is one of the province's most famous players.

- Current Lions coach and former Ireland manager Warren Gatland took the reins for the 1997 season.

- Connacht have never won the Irish Interprovincial Championship outright. They have, however, shared the Championship on three occasions in its fifty-four-year history.

- They were European Challenge Cup semi-finalists on two occasions, in 2005 and 2010.

- In November 2011 Connacht made their first-ever Heineken Cup appearance. This was courtesy of Leinster winning the 2011 Heineken Cup, which gave an extra place to an Irish team.

- Connacht lost their first five pool matches in the 2011–12 competition. They then caused a major upset when they defeated table-topping London outfit Harlequins 9–8 in their final pool game, at the Sportsground.

- Connacht's nickname is The Devil's Own. The nickname is taken from the famous 88th Regiment of Foot (Connaught Rangers), who were also dubbed The Devil's Own.

Honours

Interprovincial Championship: 3 wins

Individual Records

Top points scorer: Ian Keatley (688)
Most tries: Fionn Carr (34)
Most appearances: Michael Swift (264)

British and Irish Lions from Connacht

The following Connacht players have represented the British and Irish Lions:

Ray McLoughlin: 1966, 1971; John O'Driscoll: 1980, 1983; Ciaran Fitzgerald (captain): 1983.

Connacht Players Who Have Represented Ireland

The following Connacht players have represented Ireland at full international level:

Stephen Blake-Knox, Tony Buckley, Kieran Campbell, Victor Costello, Sean Cronin, Johnny Dooley, Gavin Duffy, Pat Duignan, Eric Elwood, Ciaran Fitzgerald, Jerry Flannery, Simon Geoghegan, Brendan Guerin, Robbie Henshaw, Bernard Jackman, Ian Keatley, Ronan Loughney, Charles Lydon, Noel Mannion, Mike McCarthy, Conor McGuinness, Mark McHugh, Ray McLoughlin, Matt Mostyn, John Muldoon, Johnny O'Connor, John O'Driscoll, Tony O'Sullivan, Eoin Reddan, Richard 'Dickie' Roche, Jim Staples and Tom Tierney.

ULSTER RUGBY

– The Ulster Branch of the IRFU was founded in 1879.

– They have won the Interprovincial Championship a record twenty-six times.

– They made history by becoming the first Irish side to win the Heineken Cup, which they won in 1999 by beating French side US Colomiers at Lansdowne Road in Dublin. The Ulster squad contained many part-time players, including Andy Matchett and Stephen McKinty, who both started the final. The team was coached by Harry Williams and managed by John Kinnear.

–   From 2001–04 Ulster were coached by Alan Solomons, a former assistant coach of the Springboks and head coach of the Stormers in his native South Africa. Under Solomons Ulster had a three-year unbeaten home record in the Heineken Cup.

–   Ulster won the inaugural Celtic Cup on 20 December 2003, beating Edinburgh in a rain-soaked final at Murrayfield. Just a month later, Ulster humbled English giants Leicester by a massive 33–0 margin in the Heineken Cup.

–   In the 2003–04 season Ulster finished second in the Celtic League, agonisingly overtaken by Llanelli on the final day of the season.

–   In the 2006 season Ulster again led the Celtic League for most of the season. However, a slump in performance, combined with a late surge from Leinster, meant that both sides were in the running to clinch the title in the final game of the season. With only four minutes left in Ulster's final match against the Ospreys, Ulster trailed by one point. David Humphreys kicked a 40-metre drop goal to win the game and the league for Ulster.

–   Ulster play their home games at Ravenhill in Belfast. Ulster first played at the ground in the 1923–24 season.

– A new stand was opened in 2009 in Ravenhill and further redevelopment was started in 2012. This was completed in early 2014 and the stadium was officially reopened in May 2014 at a Rabo Direct Pro12 match against Leinster. The new ground has a capacity of 18,196 and is now capable of hosting European Rugby Champions Cup quarter-finals and Pro12 finals. It was renamed Kingspan Stadium.

– The Ulster Ravens represent Ulster in the British and Irish Cup and in the Interprovincial Championship.

– Ravenhill has hosted two Rugby World Cup matches and several Ireland matches.

– In 2003 Ulster changed their crest. The red hand of Ulster is still in the centre of the crest but is now encircled by the outline of two rugby balls, one black, one red.

– Ulster's Robin Thompson and Willie John McBride both captained the British and Irish Lions.

– David Humphreys is Ulster's record points scorer in the Heineken Cup. He notched up 564 points between 1998 and 2008. Humphreys also holds the appearance record in that competition, having turned out fifty-seven times.

Honours

Heineken Cup/Champions Cup (1): 1999 (runners-up: 2012)

Celtic League/Magners League/Pro12 (1): 2006 (runners-up: 2004, 2013)

Celtic Cup (1): 2004

Interprovincial Championships: 26 wins

Individual Records

Top points scorer: David Humphreys (1,350)

Most tries: Andrew Trimble (64)

Most appearances: Paddy Wallace (189)

British and Irish Lions from Ulster

The following Ulster players have also represented the British and Irish Lions:

Alexander Roulston Foster: 1910; Tommy Smyth: 1910; Robert Alexander: 1938; Paddy Mayne: 1938; Jack Kyle: 1950; Cecil Pedlow: 1955; Robin Thompson: 1955; Raymond Hunter: 1962; Willie John McBride: 1962, 1966, 1968, 1971, 1974; Syd Millar: 1962, 1968; Mike Gibson: 1966, 1968, 1971, 1974, 1977; Roger Young: 1966, 1968; Stewart McKinney: 1974; Richard Milliken: 1974; Colin Patterson: 1980; David Irwin: 1983; Trevor Ringland: 1983; Steve Smith: 1989; Eric Miller: 1997; Jeremy Davidson: 1997, 2001; Tyrone Howe: 2001; Stephen

Ferris: 2009; Tommy Bowe: 2009, 2013; Rory Best: 2013; Tom Court: 2013.

ESTIMATED NUMBER OF PLAYERS IN EACH PROVINCE

	Ulster	Munster	Leinster	Connacht	Total
Senior men	7,056	5,923	10,154	2,307	25,440
Senior women	744	751	1,140	129	2,764

THE RUGBY WORLD CUP

- No team has ever retained the Rugby World Cup, which was first held in 1987.

- The winners are awarded the William Webb Ellis Cup, named after William Webb Ellis, a pupil at Rugby School who, according to legend, invented rugby by picking up the ball during a football game and running with it.

- Eden Park in Auckland, New Zealand, is the only stadium to have hosted the Rugby World Cup final twice, in 1987 and 2011. Both finals held there were won by the All Blacks.

- There were no conversions in a Rugby World Cup final between Matt Burke's for Australia in 1999 and François Trinh-Duc's for France in 2011. Jonny Wilkinson (England) and Elton Flatley (Australia) failed with their sole conversion attempts in 2003 and there were no tries in the 2007 final.

- France has never won the Rugby World Cup. They have been runners-up twice, in 1987 and 1999. They have also reached three semi-finals, in 1995, 2003 and 2007.

- No team has won a Tri Nations tournament and the Rugby World Cup in the same year.

- Three players have twice been on teams that won the Rugby World Cup – John Eales and Tim Horan for Australia, and Os Du Randt for the Springboks.

- South Africa failed to score a try in either of their Rugby World Cup finals but won both matches.

- Brendan Venter of South Africa made headlines for all the wrong reasons in the 1999 Rugby World Cup. He received a red card for stamping against Uruguay in the pool stages. He was replaced by Pieter Muller for the rest of the tournament.

- The highest ever winning margin in a World Cup match was when Australia beat Namibia 142–0 in 2003. This included a record twenty-two tries.

- Grant Fox of New Zealand has the record for the highest number of points scored in a Rugby World Cup tournament, amassing 120 in 1987.

- New Zealand have scored over a century three times: in 1995 against Japan (145–17), in 1999 against Italy (101–3), and in 2007 against Portugal (108–13).

- Jonny Wilkinson, with 15 points in 2003 and a further 6 in 2007, is the only player to have scored points in two Rugby World Cup finals.

- Simon Culhane of New Zealand holds the record for the most points scored in a Rugby World Cup match. The fly-half scored 45 points against Japan in 1995. The record for the most conversions in a match is also held by Culhane. He notched up twenty in the same match.

- The record for the most drop goals scored in a single tournament is held by Jonny Wilkinson of England, with eight in 2003.

- The oldest player to appear in a World Cup final is Brad Thorn of New Zealand, who was thirty-six years and 262 days old when he was on the team that played against France on 23 October 2011.

- The oldest player to appear in a World Cup match is Diego Ormaechea of Uruguay, who was forty years and twenty-six days old when he was on the team that played against South Africa on 15 October 1999.

- The youngest player to win a World Cup medal is François Steyn of South Africa. He was twenty years and 159 days old when South Africa won against England on 20 October 2007.

- The youngest player to score a try in a World Cup game is George North of Wales. He was nineteen years and 166 days old when he scored two tries against Namibia on 26 September 2011.

- The youngest player to appear in a World Cup final is Jonah Lomu of New Zealand, who was twenty years and forty-three days old when his team played South Africa on 24 June 1995.

- Marc Ellis of New Zealand scored the most tries in a single match, notching up six against Japan in 1995.

- Grant Fox of New Zealand holds the record for the most conversions in a World Cup tournament. He achieved thirty in 1987.

- Three teams have won the trophy twice: Australia, New Zealand and South Africa.

- Of the seven tournaments that have been held, all but one were won by a southern-hemisphere team. That dominance was broken only in 2003, when England beat Australia in the final.

- Ireland have reached the quarter-final stage five times but have never progressed to a semi-final.

- In 2011 New Zealand defeated France 37–17 in the group stages. When the sides met again in the final, just a single point separated them. New Zealand won 8–7.

- The 1995 final was dominated by place-kickers. Andrew Mehrtens of New Zealand scored all of his side's 12 points. Joel Stransky of South Africa scored all of their 15 points, including an extra-time drop goal, which won the tournament for the Boks.

- Uruguay claimed the twentieth and final place at the 2015 Rugby World Cup. They defeated Russia in the repechage final, on a 57–49 aggregate score.

RUGBY WORLD CUP RESULTS 1987–2011

1987 Rugby World Cup

Pool 1

	Pld	W	D	L	PF	PA	Pts
Australia	3	3	0	0	108	41	6
England	3	2	0	1	100	32	4
USA	3	1	0	2	39	99	2
Japan	3	0	0	3	48	123	0

Pool 2

	Pld	W	D	L	PF	PA	Pts
Wales	3	3	0	0	82	31	6
Ireland	3	2	0	1	84	41	4
Canada	3	1	0	2	65	90	2
Tonga	3	0	0	3	29	98	0

Pool 3

	Pld	W	D	L	PF	PA	Pts
New Zealand	3	3	0	0	190	34	6
Fiji	3	1	0	2	56	101	2
Italy	3	1	0	2	40	110	2
Argentina	3	1	0	2	49	90	2

Fiji qualified with the highest number of tries (Fiji 6, Italy 5, Argentina 4)

Pool 4

	Pld	W	D	L	PF	PA	Pts
France	3	2	1	0	145	44	5
Scotland	3	2	1	0	135	69	5
Romania	3	1	0	2	61	130	2
Zimbabwe	3	0	0	3	53	151	0

Quarter-finals
New Zealand 30, Scotland 3, Lancaster Park, Christchurch

Australia 33, Ireland 15, Concord Oval, Sydney

France 31, Fiji 16, Eden Park, Auckland

Wales 16, England 3, Ballymore, Brisbane

Semi-finals
France 30, Australia 24, Concord Oval, Sydney

New Zealand 49, Wales 6, Ballymore, Brisbane

Third-place play-off
Wales 22, Australia 21, Rotorua International Stadium, Rotorua

Final
New Zealand 29, France 9, Eden Park, Auckland

Referee: Kerry Fitzgerald (Australia)

Tries: Jones (1), Kirk (1), Berbizier (1), Kirwin (1)

Conversions: Camberabero (1), Fox (1)

Penalties: Camberabero (1)

Drop goals: Fox (1)

1991 Rugby World Cup

Pool 1
	Pld	W	D	L	PF	PA	Pts
New Zealand	3	3	0	0	95	39	9
England	3	2	0	1	85	33	7
Italy	3	1	0	2	57	76	5
USA	3	0	0	3	24	113	3

Pool 2

	Pld	W	D	L	PF	PA	Pts
Scotland	3	3	0	0	122	36	9
Ireland	3	2	0	1	102	51	7
Japan	3	1	0	2	77	87	5
Zimbabwe	3	0	0	3	31	158	3

Pool 3

	Pld	W	D	L	PF	PA	Pts
Australia	3	3	0	0	79	25	9
Western Samoa	3	2	0	1	54	34	7
Wales	3	1	0	2	32	61	5
Argentina	3	0	0	3	38	83	3

Pool 4

	Pld	W	D	L	PF	PA	Pts
France	3	3	0	0	82	25	9
Canada	3	2	0	1	45	33	7
Romania	3	1	0	2	31	64	5
Fiji	3	0	0	3	27	63	3

Quarter-finals

England 19, France 10, Parc des Princes, Paris

Scotland 28, Western Samoa 6, Murrayfield Stadium, Edinburgh

Australia 19, Ireland 18, Lansdowne Road, Dublin

New Zealand 29, Canada 13, Stadium Lille-Metropole, Villeneuve-d'Ascq

Semi-finals

England 9, Scotland 6, Murrayfield Stadium, Edinburgh

Australia 16, New Zealand 6, Lansdowne Road, Dublin

Third-place play-off

New Zealand 13, Scotland 6, Cardiff Arms Park, Cardiff

Final

Australia 12, England 6, Twickenham Stadium, London

Referee: Derek Bevan (Wales)

Tries: Daly (1)

Conversions: Lynagh (1)

Penalties: Webb (2), Lynagh (2)

Drop goals: 0

1995 World Cup

Pool A

	Pld	W	D	L	PF	PA	Pts
South Africa	3	3	0	0	68	26	9
Australia	3	2	0	1	87	41	7
Canada	3	1	0	2	45	50	5
Romania	3	0	0	3	14	97	3

Pool B

	Pld	W	D	L	PF	PA	Pts
England	3	3	0	0	95	60	9
Western Samoa	3	2	0	1	96	88	7
Italy	3	1	0	2	69	94	5
Argentina	3	0	0	3	69	87	3

Pool C

	Pld	W	D	L	PF	PA	Pts
New Zealand	3	3	0	0	222	45	9
Ireland	3	2	0	1	93	94	7
Wales	3	1	0	2	89	68	5
Japan	3	0	0	3	55	252	3

Pool D

	Pld	W	D	L	PF	PA	Pts
France	3	3	0	0	114	47	9
Scotland	3	2	0	1	149	27	7
Tonga	3	1	0	2	44	90	5
Ivory Coast	3	0	0	3	29	172	3

Quarter-finals

France 36, Ireland 12, Kings Park Stadium, Durban

South Africa 42, Western Samoa 14, Ellis Park Stadium, Johannesburg

England 25, Australia 22, Newlands Cricket Ground, Cape Town

New Zealand 48, Scotland 30, Loftus Versfeld Stadium, Pretoria

Semi-finals

South Africa 19, France 15, Kings Park Stadium, Durban

New Zealand 45, England 29, Newlands Cricket Ground, Cape Town

Third-place play-off

France 19, England 9, Loftus Versfeld Stadium, Pretoria

Final

South Africa 15, New Zealand 12 (a.e.t.)*, Ellis Park, Johannesburg

Referee: Ed Morrison (England)

Tries: 0

Conversions: 0

Penalties: Stransky (3), Mehrtens (3)

Drop goals: Stransky (2), Mehrtens (1)

*a.e.t. = after extra time

1999 Rugby World Cup

Pool A

	Pld	W	D	L	PF	PA	Pts
South Africa	3	3	0	0	132	35	9
Scotland	3	2	0	1	120	58	7
Uruguay	3	1	0	2	42	97	5
Spain	3	0	0	3	18	122	3

Pool B

	Pld	W	D	L	PF	PA	Pts
New Zealand	3	3	0	0	176	28	9
England	3	2	0	1	184	47	7
Tonga	3	1	0	2	47	171	5
Italy	3	0	0	3	35	196	3

Pool C

	Pld	W	D	L	PF	PA	Pts
France	3	3	0	0	108	52	9
Fiji	3	2	0	1	124	68	7
Canada	3	1	0	2	114	82	5
Namibia	3	0	0	3	42	186	3

Pool D

	Pld	W	D	L	PF	PA	Pts
Wales	3	2	0	1	118	71	7
Samoa	3	2	0	1	97	72	7
Argentina	3	2	0	1	83	51	7
Japan	3	0	0	3	36	140	3

Pool E

	Pld	W	D	L	PF	PA	Pts
Australia	3	3	0	0	135	31	9
Ireland	3	2	0	1	100	45	7
Romania	3	1	0	2	50	126	5
USA	3	0	0	3	52	135	3

Quarter-finals*

Australia 24, Wales 9, Millennium Stadium, Cardiff

South Africa 44, England 21, Stade de France, Saint-Denis

New Zealand 30, Scotland 18, Murrayfield, Edinburgh

France 47, Argentina 26, Lansdowne Road, Dublin

Semi-finals

Australia 27, South Africa 21 (a.e.t.), Twickenham Stadium, London

France 43, New Zealand 31, Twickenham Stadium, London

Third-place play-off

South Africa 22, New Zealand 18, Millennium Stadium, Cardiff

*Because there were five pools in this World Cup, play-offs were played to determine who would reach the quarter-finals.

Final
Australia 35, France 12, Millennium Stadium, Cardiff

Referee: André Watson (South Africa)

Tries: Finegan (1), Tune (1)

Conversions: Burke (2)

Penalties: Lamaison (4), Burke (7)

Drop goals: 0

2003 Rugby World Cup

Pool A

	Pld	W	D	L	PF	PA	Pts
Australia	4	4	0	0	273	32	18
Ireland	4	3	0	1	141	56	15
Argentina	4	2	0	2	140	57	11
Romania	4	1	0	3	65	192	5
Namibia	4	0	0	4	28	310	0

Pool B

	Pld	W	D	L	PF	PA	Pts
France	4	4	0	0	204	70	20
Scotland	4	3	0	1	102	97	14
Fiji	4	2	0	2	98	114	10
USA	4	1	0	3	86	125	6
Japan	4	0	0	4	79	163	0

Pool C

	Pld	W	D	L	PF	PA	Pts
England	4	4	0	0	255	47	19
South Africa	4	3	0	1	184	60	15

Samoa	4	2	0	2	138	117	10
Uruguay	4	1	0	3	56	255	4
Georgia	4	0	0	4	46	200	0

Pool D

	Pld	W	D	L	PF	PA	Pts
New Zealand	4	4	0	0	282	57	20
Wales	4	3	0	1	132	98	14
Italy	4	2	0	2	77	123	8
Canada	4	1	0	3	54	135	5
Tonga	4	0	0	4	46	178	1

Quarter-finals

New Zealand 29, South Africa 9, Telstra Dome, Melbourne

Australia 33, Scotland 16, Suncorp Stadium, Brisbane

France 43, Ireland 21, Telstra Dome, Melbourne

England 28, Wales 16, Suncorp Stadium, Brisbane

Semi-finals

Australia 22, New Zealand 10, Telstra Stadium, Sydney

England 24, France 7, Telstra Stadium, Sydney

Third-place play-off

New Zealand 40, France 13, Telstra Stadium, Sydney

Final

England 20, Australia 17 (a.e.t.), Telstra Stadium, Sydney

Referee: André Watson (South Africa)

Tries: Tuqiri (1), Robinson (1)

Conversions: 0

Penalties: Wilkinson (4), Flatley (4)

Drop goals: Wilkinson (1)

2007 Rugby World Cup

Pool A

	Pld	W	D	L	PF	PA	Pts
South Africa	4	4	0	0	189	47	19
England	4	3	0	1	108	88	14
Tonga	4	2	0	2	89	96	9
Samoa	4	1	0	3	69	143	5
USA	4	0	0	4	61	142	1

Pool B

	Pld	W	D	L	PF	PA	Pts
Australia	4	4	0	0	215	41	20
Fiji	4	3	0	1	114	136	15
Wales	4	2	0	2	168	105	12
Japan	4	0	1	3	64	210	3
Canada	4	0	1	3	51	120	2

Pool C

	Pld	W	D	L	PF	PA	Pts
New Zealand	4	4	0	0	309	35	20
Scotland	4	3	0	1	116	66	14
Italy	4	2	0	2	85	117	9
Romania	4	1	0	3	40	161	5
Portugal	4	0	0	4	38	209	1

Pool D

	Pld	W	D	L	PF	PA	Pts
Argentina	4	4	0	0	143	33	18
France	4	3	0	1	188	37	15
Ireland	4	2	0	2	64	82	9
Georgia	4	1	0	3	50	111	5
Namibia	4	0	0	4	30	212	0

Quarter-finals
England 12, Australia 10, Stade Vélodrome, Marseille

France 20, New Zealand 18, Millennium Stadium, Cardiff

South Africa 37, Fiji 20, Stade Vélodrome, Marseille

Argentina 19, Scotland 13, Stade de France, Saint-Denis

Semi-finals
England 14, France 9, Stade de France, Saint-Denis

South Africa 37, Argentina 13, Stade de France, Saint-Denis

Third-place play-off
Argentina 34, France 10, Parc des Princes, Paris

Final
South Africa 15, England 6, Stade de France, Saint-Denis

Referee: Alain Rolland (Ireland)

Tries: 0

Conversions: 0

Penalties: Montgomery (4), Wilkinson (2), Steyn (1)

Drop goals: 0

2011 Rugby World Cup

Pool A

	Pld	W	D	L	PF	PA	Pts
New Zealand	4	4	0	0	240	49	20
France	4	2	0	2	124	96	11
Tonga	4	2	0	2	80	98	9
Canada	4	1	1	2	82	168	6
Japan	4	0	1	3	69	184	2

Pool B

	Pld	W	D	L	PF	PA	Pts
England	4	4	0	0	137	34	18
Argentina	4	3	0	1	90	40	14
Scotland	4	2	0	2	73	59	11
Georgia	4	1	0	3	48	90	4
Romania	4	0	0	4	44	169	0

Pool C

	Pld	W	D	L	PF	PA	Pts
Ireland	4	4	0	0	135	34	17
Australia	4	3	0	1	173	48	15
Italy	4	2	0	2	92	95	10
USA	4	1	0	3	38	122	4
Russia	4	0	0	4	57	196	1

Pool D

	Pld	W	D	L	PF	PA	Pts
South Africa	4	4	0	0	166	24	18
Wales	4	3	0	1	180	34	15
Samoa	4	2	0	2	91	49	10
Fiji	4	1	0	3	59	167	5
Namibia	4	0	0	4	44	266	0

Quarter-finals

Wales 22, Ireland 10, Wellington Regional Stadium, Wellington

France 19, England 12, Eden Park, Auckland

Australia 11, South Africa 9, Wellington Regional Stadium, Wellington

New Zealand 33, Argentina 10, Eden Park, Auckland

Semi-finals

France 9, Wales 8, Eden Park, Auckland

New Zealand 20, Australia 6, Eden Park, Auckland

Third-Place play-off

Australia 21, Wales 18, Eden Park, Auckland

Final

New Zealand 8, France 7, Eden Park, Auckland

Referee: Craig Joubert (South Africa)

Tries: Dusautoir (1), Woodcock (1)

Conversions: Trinh-Duc (1)

Penalties: Donald (1)

Drop goals: 0

IRELAND'S WORLD CUP HISTORY

– Ireland have competed at every Rugby World Cup tournament. The furthest they have progressed is the quarter-finals, which they have made five times out of seven attempts.

- Ireland have never played England or South Africa in the Rugby World Cup.

- In the first tournament, held in Australia and New Zealand in 1987, Ireland finished second in their pool after a loss to Wales. Ireland were knocked out by Australia in the quarter-final in Sydney.

- In 1991 Ireland again lost one match in the pool stages, to neighbours Scotland. Ireland again met Australia in the quarter-finals, losing by one point.

- In 1995 the Irish were runners-up in their pool to the All Blacks. Ireland were defeated by France in the quarter-final in Durban.

- In 1999 Ireland finished second in the pool stages, behind Australia. They went into the quarter-final play-offs, a new system introduced in the 1999 tournament, where they lost to Argentina. Under the new system they were not given automatic entry into the 2003 tournament.

- In the 2003 qualifying matches, Ireland defeated Russia and Georgia to reach the finals. Ireland finished second to Australia in their pool and were knocked out by the French in the quarter-finals.

- In the 2007 World Cup Ireland were placed in the so-called 'group of death', along with hosts France, Argentina, Namibia and Georgia. Their progress was put in jeopardy when they failed to earn a bonus point in a 14–10 win over Georgia.

Ireland then lost to France 25–3. Entering their last group match against Argentina, they needed four tries to secure a bonus point. They were defeated 30–15 and crashed out at the pool stage for the first time.

– Ireland were paired with Australia, Russia, USA and Italy in Pool C for the 2011 Rugby World Cup. Ireland's second pool game was against Australia. Despite being the underdogs, Ireland recorded their first victory over Australia in a World Cup, with a 15–6 win. They then secured first place in the pool with a 36–6 win over Italy, the first time that Ireland were group winners in their World Cup history. Ireland then lost an all-European quarter-final to Wales 10–22.

AMAZING RUGBY TALES

EVERYONE A WINNER

The Five Nations championship of 1973 produced a result that stands alone in the record books as the most amazing of all time.

When Wales destroyed England 25–9 at the Cardiff Arms Park on 20 January, the championship looked to be anything but close and the English looked like anything but possible champions. The Welsh lived up to their billing as tournament favourites, with an all-star cast including J. P. R. Williams, Gerald Davies, Phil Bennett and Gareth Edwards. After this performance, hopes were not high for the Scots when the Welsh visited Murrayfield a fortnight later. The Scottish, however, managed to edge a tense match 10–9. Then Ireland downed England 18–9 at Lansdowne Road and it seemed to be the end of the road for the English, who faced France in their next match.

The French had started with a hard-fought win over Scotland, and the English game seemed to provide them with the ideal platform to make a real statement of intent. Although the English faithful packed Twickenham on the day, they believed they had come to witness the burial of their Five Nations aspirations.

However, the English team hadn't bothered to read the script and rose from the ashes to stun Les

Bleus with a brace of tries from David Duckham. When Wales beat Ireland 16–12, they led the championship with four points, but Ireland, with Mike Gibson in imperious form, remained very firmly in the hunt.

Then the topsy-turvy title race delivered another seismic shock when Scotland took full advantage of their home comforts, prevailing 19–14 over a strangely lethargic Ireland. This meant that going into the final round of matches, it seemed only Wales or France could claim the spoils.

The Welsh were – dare we say it? – red-hot favourites to beat France and clinch the crown. But the French spoiled the party with a 12–3 scoreline. Wales' Phil Bennett left his kicking boots at home and would rue missing four shots at goal.

This left France to travel to Dublin the following month, where a single point would give them the title. In a championship where the only expected result was the unexpected, there had been one thing that had remained consistent: all the matches in the tournament had resulted in wins for the home side. An Irish victory would make it a perfect ten out of ten for the home teams. It also provided one of the most astonishing climaxes in rugby union history.

The tournament organisers clutched their rosary beads a little tighter as the sands of time ebbed away in Dublin. With Ireland leading by six points to four, Jean-Pierre Romeu had an opportunity to finally end the logjam at the top of the Five Nations table, but the French out-half fluffed his chance and Ireland held on.

While there is an old sporting adage that says the table never lies, it certainly didn't ring true on this occasion. Wales topped the table with the best scoring average, with England finishing in last place, but all the teams were on four points. There were no tiebreakers in those days, so only the final points were taken into account. In the end all five competing nations were declared champions!

LIFE OF O'REILLY

When Tony O'Reilly was recalled to the Irish side in 1970 after a seven-year absence, he arrived at training in a chauffeur-driven Rolls Royce, to the astonishment of his teammates. He headed for the dressing room, while his driver followed behind him, trying his best not to drop any of O'Reilly's kit bags.

O'Reilly was a winger who knew how to score tries. A British and Irish Lion, he had played fifteen games during the 1955 tour, scoring sixteen tries. This included a hat-trick against a North Eastern Districts XV on 20 July and another against Transvaal on 23 July. He also played in all four Tests against South Africa, making his Test debut on the right wing in front of a crowd of 95,000 at Ellis Park on 6 August. He scored a try in the Lions 23–22 victory. In 1959 he scored twenty-one tries in twenty-one games played.

The man who would go on to be the richest businessman in Ireland returned to the fold as a last-minute replacement in the Five Nations game against

England at Twickenham on 14 February 1970. On a wet and horrible day in the English capital, his form failed to appear – O'Reilly had a miserable outing in the green jersey. This would be the final appearance for the 'Rolls Royce of Irish wingers'.

Interestingly, his late call-up had been at the expense of one Frank O'Driscoll. O'Driscoll had played in a couple of non-Test matches for Ireland and had been knocking at the door of a full Irish international cap. O'Reilly's inclusion spelled the end of his Irish involvement and he never won that elusive Test place. However, the O'Driscoll family name would later make a greater impact on Irish rugby than O'Reilly did. Frank's son, Brian, would go on to become a rugby legend and was the most capped rugby player of all time at his retirement in 2014.

ONE-WAY TICKET

In 1924–25 the All Blacks toured Great Britain, Ireland, Canada and France with a team nicknamed 'The Invincibles', playing test matches against Ireland, Wales, England and France. With them came a stuffed Kiwi bird in a specially designed wooden travelling case, the perfect mascot for the All Blacks touring team. However, despite travelling on a one-way ticket, the mascot remained in its box and was never presented to the opposition. Instead it made the long journey back to New Zealand.

The All Blacks had intended to give the bird to the

first team to beat them on their tour. It was expected that a punishing schedule of thirty-two tour matches would provide ample opportunity for one of their opponents to conquer the mighty team and win the mascot. But amazingly New Zealand's opponents failed to muster a single victory, as 'The Invincibles' lived up to their name. Overall the team scored 838 points and conceded only 116.

The New Zealand team was initially captained by Cliff Porter, although an injury restricted him to seventeen games. Vice-captain Jock Richardson then took over the captain's duties for the remainder of the tour. The team included some of the giants of New Zealand rugby, including Cyril and Maurice Brownlie and the legendary George Nēpia. Nēpia lined out for the Kiwis in all thirty-two tour matches, on a tour which started in September 1924 and ended in February 1925.

With no victor to present the mascot to, the Kiwi returned home again with its triumphant teammates and supporters. It has never taken flight since. It stands proudly in the New Zealand Rugby Museum, a symbol of one of rugby's greatest-ever touring sides.

GASTRONOMIC MISTAKE

When Gaston Vareilles assembled with the rest of his French team members in 1910, he seemed destined for a long and distinguished international rugby career with Les Bleus. Sadly for Gaston, his stomach had other ideas! He was troubled by a rumbling in his stomach on the way to the train's first port of call, Lyon. Gaston could not resist his gastronomic urges any longer. The train halted briefly for a comfort stop at Lyon, and Gaston headed for the nearest sandwich vendor.

Fate served up more than just a sandwich to the hungry son of France. Gaston had just purchased the precious bounty when he heard a mournful siren call from the departing train. Showing himself to be fleet of foot, he ran down the platform in a desperate attempt to board the train, but failed to make it. As he sat down to contemplate this cruel twist of fate, he had more than a sandwich to digest. The French International Rugby Board took a very dim view of Gaston's match-day mishap. It proved to be the end of his career before it started. He was never again selected to play for his country.

THE ALL BLUES

The silver fern that adorns the black jersey of the All Blacks is a badge of honour like no other for New Zealand players. And yet, while it may be hard to believe, when New Zealand first played overseas, they sported dark-blue rugby jerseys with a simple, hand-stitched, gold fern leaf. After the first 'outsiders' (New South Wales) toured the country in 1882, the 'golden Kiwi' colonials returned the visit two years later, wearing this jersey emblem and demolishing the opposition on Australian soil.

In 1902 Thomas Rangiwahia Ellison, also known as Tom or Tamati Erihana, penned one of the earliest books on New Zealand rugby, *The Art of Rugby Football*. A true rugby pioneer, Tom Ellison devised the indigenous 2-3-2 scrum and wing-forward position. He was also a member of the 1888–89 Native team and captained and coached the very first New Zealand rugby team.

For all his glittering achievements, it could be argued that Ellison's greatest contribution came at the first annual New Zealand Rugby Football Union meeting in 1893. There he successfully put forward the motion that the national uniform should comprise a black jersey with a silver fern, based on the uniform worn by the Native team he played for. The All Blues were thus consigned to rugby history, and the legend of the All Blacks was born.

THE NATIONAL ANTHEM IS BORN

The singing of a country's national anthem before an international fixture is now an integral part of the pre-match preliminaries. Sung with pride and passion by players and supporters alike, it is a reminder of where we come from. Yet the first time a national anthem was sung before a sporting event happened by accident rather than design.

On 16 November 1905 New Zealand took on Wales at Cardiff Arms Park. The All Blacks, as is the tradition, performed their ferocious haka before the start of the game. The traditional Maori war dance is often seen as an attempt to intimidate the opposition. However, this time, after the New Zealand players had finished the haka, the Welsh players responded by beginning to sing their national anthem, 'Hen Wlad Fy Nhadau' ('Old Land of My Fathers'). A few supporters started to join in with the players and the song began to ripple around the stadium. More and more voices joined in the chorus. Slowly but surely the song rose to a crescendo. By the end of the song a tradition had been born.

The words *Hen wlad fy nhadau* are the first line of a traditional Welsh song written by Evan James, and the tune was composed by his son, James James, in 1856. The singing, which began as an act of defiance by the Welsh, is now part and parcel of world rugby and sporting culture.

'ACE' RUGBY FORWARD

Frank Owen Stoker, who was born on 29 May 1867, is the holder of a unique sporting record: he is the only rugby international to have won at Wimbledon.

Stoker was the Irish doubles tennis champion with his partner Joshua Pim in 1890, 1891 and 1893–95. In 1890 and 1893 he and Pim also won the doubles title at Wimbledon. A member of the Lansdowne Lawn Tennis Club, Stoker was ranked among the top ten doubles players in the world in 1892. He also played five times in the Irish rugby union team between 1886 and 1891. A forward, he lined out in four matches in the Home Nations Championship and once against the New Zealand Natives.

When not excelling in his sporting life, Stoker trained as a dental surgeon and qualified at the Royal College of Surgeons of Ireland. He also had a connection with a very famous literary figure. A cousin of Bram Stoker, the creator of Count Dracula, Frank probably neglected to mention that fact to any of the patients attending his surgery!

BACK TO THE FUTURE

The jerseys worn by the Original All Blacks touring party in 1905 were certainly original in design. Despite being fashioned over a century ago, the famous jersey bears a startling resemblance to the modern high-performance jerseys of the professional era. Manufactured by Manawatu Knitting Mills, it was collarless, almost skin-tight and was made from fine wool with a quilted, waxed linen yoke (to repel water) around the shoulders. The neck was edged with leather and the jersey was laced up the front.

The Original All Blacks (also known simply as 'The Originals') toured the British Isles, France and the United States in 1905–06. Their opening game was on 16 September 1905 against Devon and they won easily with a scoreline of 55–4. The new-look jerseys caused almost as much surprise as the visiting New Zealand team. Such was the shock of Devon's defeat that some newspapers in Britain reported that it was Devon that scored 55 points and not the All Blacks.

The Originals went on to defeat every English side they faced, including a 16–3 victory over English county champions Durham, and a 32–0 victory over Blackheath. They defeated Scotland, Ireland and England, with the closest of the three matches their 12–7 victory over Scotland. The team's only loss of the tour was a 3–0 defeat by Wales at Cardiff Arms Park. They tasted victory in thirty-four out of thirty-five matches. The visitors scored 976 points and conceded only 59, ensuring that the visiting Originals would live long in the memory, and not just for their sense of fashion!

GRAND SLAM

In 1948 the world was slowly returning to normality after the devastation of the Second World War. NASA was preparing the launch of its first attempt to put a primate, a rhesus monkey named Albert, in space. Back in Ireland the national rugby team of '48 was also about to embark on a journey which would end in sporting immortality.

The term 'Grand Slam' did not exist in 1948. For Irish players the Triple Crown was the Holy Grail. Victory over England, Scotland and Wales constituted this elusive feat. The last Irish success had been in 1899, almost fifty years previously. A winning start was imperative. A loss in the opening leg of the triple-header almost rendered the season meaningless.

The games against France were almost a separate entity for Ireland at the time. They were normally played in January, before Ireland's other three matches. The players also faced a very different set of challenges. The logistics alone of an away game could be a nightmare. For this game in 1948, which was at the Colombes ground in Paris, Jack Kyle had to travel from Belfast to Dublin, then on to Holyhead, London, Dover, Calais and finally Paris. It was a gruelling trip of almost two days. The journey didn't end there, however. A trip to the Folies Bergère the night before the game added even more mileage to the epic voyage.

The French, as ever, presented a difficult challenge on home soil, but Ireland came out with fire in their bellies. They started, in rugby parlance, firmly on the front foot, attacking the hosts with a furious intensity. Tries from centre Paddy Reid, debutant Jim McCarthy and wing Barney Mullan ensured a famous 13–6 victory and shortened the long road home.

With the French out of the way, Ireland could now plan for the bigger picture. Up next were old foes England, at Twickenham. Ireland had beaten them 22–0 in the previous season's fixture and were out of the traps quickly, racing into an 11-point lead. Kyle went on to be the shining light of that season, though an error he made when passing allowed an interception, gifting England a try. Dickie Guest gratefully accepted the present and raced away to score. Ireland had to dig deep and they scraped home on an 11–10 scoreline.

Scotland came to Lansdowne Road next and, after

a hard-fought encounter, Ireland prevailed 6–0. Kyle and Barney Mullan both crossed the try line, as the Scots dug into the trenches in a real war of attrition. The final leg, against the Welsh in Belfast, was at the spiritual home of Ulster rugby, Ravenhill. Before 1954 not all Irish games were played in Dublin.

The players in those days learned of their selection on Radio Athlone the Sunday before the match. In the 1950s, training consisted of a single session. This would last for half an hour on the Friday afternoon preceding the game. Kyle was grateful for the opportunity to sleep at home the night before the contest.

Thirty thousand people gathered in Ulster that day as the history books were rewritten. Motorists from the Republic required special permission to cross the border. This process could take weeks, so many supporters had an anxious wait as they waded through the necessary documentation.

The Irish had been in this position many times before. On eight previous occasions Wales had denied Ireland a Triple Crown on the last day, the most recent being in Swansea the previous year, and a staggering six times in twelve seasons. The Irish knew the Welsh dragons would spit fire and fury. It was not a day for the faint-hearted.

Following the kick-off Karl Mullen, the Irish captain, received some rough treatment as fists flew and curses were uttered. Ireland responded by targeting Welsh scrum-half Haydn Tanner. Ireland hit the front when Barney Mullan crashed over. Bleddyn Williams, who was regarded as the original Prince of Centres, responded for Wales with an accomplished individual effort. The dragons' tails were now firmly up, and nerves began to jangle in the enthralled crowd.

The next score would have a critical bearing on the outcome. Ireland tried to unsettle Welsh full-back Frank Trott. This tactic would reap a rich dividend. Trott, an undertaker by trade, sounded the death knell for his own team's ambitions when he fumbled the ball. Des O'Brien picked it up and charged up field, making tracks for the Welsh line. John 'Jack' Daly was in tow and finished the move. He had spent the Second World War hauling wireless equipment around northern Italy. He used haulage skills of a different variety here and carried half of Wales over the line with him! Daly, a prop who always did a somersault upon entering the pitch, now had the home supporters doing somersaults of their own. The Welsh fire had been extinguished.

At the death, bloodied and battered green-shirted heroes raised heavy arms into the evening sky. The men of '48 could never have imagined the legacy of that day. The clean sweep that they so bravely achieved would in time take on mythical proportions. The team would go down in rugby history as Ireland's first Grand Slam winners and they would remain the only Irish team to lay claim to this victory until the hard-fought and nerve-shredding win, once again against determined Welsh foes, in 2009.

The men of '48 will always retain a special place in

Irish rugby folklore. Highlight reels still spirit us back there. Sepia images pay homage to the greatness of that band of sporting brothers on the road to immortality.

THE GHOST IN THE PICTURE

The most famous rugby painting of all time hangs on the wall of the President's Suite in the West Stand of Twickenham Stadium. The painting has confounded rugby historians for over a century and poses a burning question: who is the ghost in the picture?

The painting is of a late-nineteenth-century match between two of England's fiercest rivals, Lancashire and Yorkshire. The two counties, which had famously fought the War of the Roses, were at the time of the painting the dominant forces in English rugby. The painting is by William Barnes Wollen R.A. (1857–1936), a portrait painter who produced a number of rugby paintings and a large number of specially commissioned war canvases. It was completed in 1895 and was hung in the Royal Academy the following year. It then vanished for more than sixty years, before reappearing in a second-hand shop in Grey Street, Newcastle, in 1957.

The mystery of the painting concerns the existence of a ghost player who was in the original version but was then painted out. This strange fact emerged when the RFU had the painting cleaned after it came into their possession in the late 1960s.

The burning question is: why was one of the Yorkshire players removed from the painting? Conspiracy theories abound. During the 1890s the RFU was strongly opposed to anyone who attempted to change the amateur game. George Rowland Hill was a powerful administrator and had issued many warnings that he would not tolerate payment of players. All the players in the portrait defected to the Northern Rugby Football Union, which led to the breakaway code of rugby league. But if the players had defected en masse, why was just one singled out and removed from the portrait?

Another theory is that the player was deliberately painted out for failing to pay for the privilege of inclusion. However, that is unlikely, though it does lead to the third theory, which concerns the positioning of the ghost player. Overlapping his position on the field is the match referee, who has been given the features of Rowland Hill. (Spectators and linesmen have also been given the features of RFU officials of the time.) Could the artist have sought to gain favour by highlighting Rowland Hill and removing the nearest player?

All of this is speculation, and it is doubtful the truth will ever emerge, nor is it likely the identity of the player who has been painted out of the game's history will ever be revealed. Like his image in the painting, the Yorkshire man has now vanished into the mists of time.

This was not the only rugby painting to include

a mysterious figure, but in the case of the painting of a little girl dressed in full Springbok rugby kit and holding a rugby ball, the identity of the protagonist would eventually be revealed.

The oil painting, discovered in a house clearance in Wales, was purchased in 1998 at auction and initially confounded rugby experts worldwide. The artist's name was indecipherable. Badly damaged and needing extensive restoration, it dated from 1907, a time when no girls were playing rugby. Because of this it was dubbed the Rugby Revelation. Who was the little Springbok girl in this extraordinary oil painting, which cost twice as much to restore as it did to buy at auction? She was most certainly not a team mascot, so where did she come from?

In this case extensive research eventually revealed that the little Springbok was, in fact, a Welsh girl named Kathleen Trick. Her father, a member of the London Welsh RFC, had been invited to a costume ball in 1907 given by the Lord Mayor of London in honour of the first touring South African side, so six-year-old Kathleen went to the party dressed in a full Springbok kit, donated by the team themselves. The amazing portrait is now housed in the World Rugby Museum.

THE COURAGEOUS LION

Tom Crean was one of Leinster's first British and Irish Lions, playing for the team in 1896. Between 1894 and 1896 he also made nine appearances for his country, and in 1894 was an integral member of the first Ireland team to win both a Home Nations Championship and a Triple Crown. In 1896 Crean helped Ireland win their second Home Nations title. His performances led to him being selected for the 1896 tour to South Africa, and he also captained the tourists in two Test matches. At the end of the tour, Crean decided not to return home, instead staying in Johannesburg, where he played with the Wanderers and worked as a doctor in one of the city's hospitals.

His bravery on the playing field would be matched by his exploits on the field of war. Crean is one of three Irish rugby union internationals to have been awarded the Victoria Cross. He enlisted as a trooper in the Imperial Light Horse when the Second Boer War broke out in South Africa in 1899, becoming the brigade's medical officer. He was wounded in the Battle of Elandslaagte in October of that year, but soon returned to the battlefield. Crean's bravery in attending to two wounded soldiers at the Battle of Tygerskloof in December won him a Victoria Cross. Despite coming under heavy fire and being wounded twice, Crean continued to attend to the men until he collapsed and was feared dead. In 1906 he retired from the army, but re-enlisted when the First World War broke out. He joined the Royal Army Medical Corps, serving with the 1st Cavalry Brigade. In June 1915 he was honoured by being made a Companion of the Distinguished Service Order. He was promoted to major on 26 February 1916 and commanded the

44th Field Ambulance, British Expeditionary Force, on the Western Front.

Later Crean spent some time as a medical officer at the hospital in the Royal Enclosure, Ascot. Crean's quick thinking was again to the fore when he performed a life-saving operation on a jockey thrown from his horse during a race. Crean removed sections of the bones of the jockey's skull with a hammer and chisel while still on the course!

Crean would ultimately pay the price for his heroism. Bad health and old injuries meant he had trouble running his private practice and he was declared bankrupt in 1922. He died from diabetes in 1923, at his home in Mayfair, London. He was aged just forty-nine. Tom Crean is buried in St Mary's R.C. Cemetery, Kensal Green. His gravestone is a small and unremarkable memorial to a truly remarkable man. This proud son of Leinster rugby was a true hero.

LYNAGH BREAKS IRISH HEARTS

Ireland has never reached the semi-final of the Rugby World Cup. Despite qualifying from the group stages, winning a last-eight match has proved to be out of reach. The closest they ever came was in 1991, against Australia, when the team were within seconds of reaching the last four of the competition.

No one genuinely believed that Ireland would push Australia for the full 80 minutes of that fateful game. The teams had played a rather one-sided encounter in the 1987 World Cup pool stages, with the Wallabies emerging comfortable winners. Moreover, Ireland had hardly set the world alight in their opening matches of the 1991 tournament. They had laboured to a win over minnows Japan and were out of sorts against Scotland at Murrayfield, going under on a 24–15 scoreline. A win over another competition minnow, Zimbabwe, left them facing the daunting challenge of playing the in-form Wallabies.

In contrast Australia had topped their pool, defeating Western Samoa, Wales and Argentina during the group stages, but the Australian coach, Bob Dwyer, was still not taking the Irish lightly. He knew an Irish team at Lansdowne Road was a dangerous animal. A proud and very passionate team, with fanatical supporters, they would test his troops to the very limit. He secretly feared a war of attrition, and Ireland duly obliged by unleashing fury upon their much vaunted opponents.

Dwyer was a very worried man as the game entered its final minutes. Australia had been unable to find their rhythm. Time and time again they had struggled to break the gain line, as the Irish tackled as if their lives depended on it. With only a few minutes left on the clock, the game was on a knife-edge. Just three points separated two totally committed teams, and the Lansdowne Road faithful were daring to dream of a victory. The Aussies, who were overwhelming favourites, poured forward looking to land a knockout blow. The Irish defended with all their might.

A rare breakaway from the men in green shirts ended the siege. Gordon Hamilton seized on a breaking ball and surged towards the Australian 25-yard line. The NIFC club man had never scored a try for his country. The home crowd rose as he charged towards what surely would be the match-clinching score. Australian cover was thin on the ground, but it was closing fast. Hamilton pumped his legs one last time as immortality beckoned. As clawing Wallaby hands grasped his jersey, he touched down after a nerve-shredding 40-metre dash. The stadium erupted; Ireland was on the verge of making Rugby World Cup history. Ralph Keyes, who had performed his kicking duties brilliantly, slotted over the conversion from the far left and the Irish had a slender three-point advantage.

It was bedlam at the old ground as the crowd and the players began to hope for a massive upset. However, the heady atmosphere left the Irish vulnerable after scoring and the Aussies would hit them with the ultimate sucker-punch. Ireland conceded a soft penalty and Michael Lynagh looked set to step up and take the penalty to level the scores. Ireland switched off for a few seconds and the Wallaby number 10 opted to take a quick tap penalty. The Irish defence scrambled to cover the gap, but Tim Horan and Jason Little combined to make up valuable ground. Little delayed for a moment before sending the ball out to David Campese, who seemed destined to score.

The crowd held their breath as the frantic Irish

cover tried desperately to hold up Campese. Somehow the retreating Irish managed to stop him inches short of the line. It seemed the cavalry would arrive and stem the Aussie tide.

The player who would go on to become Australia's record try scorer had other ideas. Teammate Michael Lynagh had tracked Campese all the way and peeled off his shoulder. The Aussie wing off-loaded the ball to Lynagh, who bounced his way over the line. An eerie silence fell upon the stadium as the Australian dagger ripped through broken Irish hearts.

It had been a close call for the Aussies, who now faced the formidable All Blacks in the semi-final. They emerged victorious there and went on to win the competition with a 12–6 defeat of England at Twickenham. For Ireland it was again a case of so near and yet so far. They have now played in seven World Cup tournaments and the wait for a last-four appearance goes on.

THE LIONS CALL 999

When the Lions were in trouble in the 1974 Test Series against South Africa, they called 999. Well, almost.

The South Africans were renowned for their robust style of play and were intent on creating mayhem at every opportunity. As the Boks attempted to soften up their British and Irish opponents, the Lions' captain, Willie John McBride, knew the only way for the tourists to win was to fight fire with fire. He called his partner, fellow lock Gordon Brown of Scotland, and they agreed on a policy of one in, all in. If a Lion was struck or intimidated, the whole team would rush to his defence.

At that time there were only substitutions if a doctor agreed that a player was physically unable to continue. There was no video ref or sideline officials to keep the punching, kicking and head-butting to a minimum.

Knowing the South Africans would continue to resort to foul play, the Lions decided to get their retaliation in first. The signal for this was to call 99, a code McBride came up with. Then the Lions would clobber their nearest rival players. Once McBride issued the call, the Lions duly obliged.

The Springboks were so surprised by the fury unleashed on them that they lost their discipline and eventually lost the series 3–0. It was the first victory by a Lions touring party in South Africa.

THE SIX NATIONS CHAMPIONSHIP

- England and Scotland clashed in the first official rugby union international, played in 1871. Over the following twelve years the English and Scots would continue to compete against each other occasionally, in friendlies. However, it was in 1883, when Ireland and Wales joined the fray, that the first Home Nations Championship was created.

- The Home Nations Championship, played between teams from England, Ireland, Scotland and Wales, was the first international rugby union tournament. The championship was played from 1883 to 1909 and again from 1932 to 1939, after France was ejected from the Five Nations for paying players.

- The Six Nations Championship is the successor to the Five Nations Championship which began in 1910 and ran to 1931 (excluding the years of 1915–19) and again from 1947 to 1999. In 2000 Italy joined the championship, which led to it being renamed the Six Nations Championship.

- France went from 1910–53 without winning the championship. Even though they didn't play in the competition for most of the 1930s, this still adds up to twenty-nine years without a win.

– England and Wales are the joint current record holders for outright wins of the Home Nations, Five Nations and Six Nations championships, with twenty-six titles each.

– The original Championship trophy was conceived by the Earl of Westmorland and first presented to the winners of the 1993 championship, France. It had fifteen side panels representing the fifteen members of the team, and three handles to represent the three officials (the referee and two touch judges). In 2015 this was replaced with a new trophy crafted by silversmiths Thomas Lyte. Its six-sided shape represents the six teams that now participate in the competition.

– Wales sit at the top of the roll of honour of wins thanks to more shared titles (12) than England (10).

– Since the Six Nations era started in 2000, only Italy and Scotland have failed to win the title.

– Since the start of the competition in 2000, Italy have finished in last place (Wooden Spoon) on ten occasions, Scotland have been last four times, in 2004, 2007, 2012 and 2015, and Wales and France have both been last once.

– Super Saturday, 21 March 2015, set a number of Six Nations records:

> Italy conceded their highest total of points in a home Six Nations game, losing to Wales by 60–21. Conversely, this was Wales' highest

ever score and their biggest victory in the Six Nations.

Twenty-seven tries and 221 points across the three games was the most scored on one day in any Six Nations competition.

Ireland equalled their biggest away win in the Six Nations, beating Scotland 40–10.

England v. France saw England concede five tries, their highest Six Nations total.

France conceded 55 points, seven tries and seven conversions in the match, all their highest Six Nations totals.

RECORDS

– Ronan O'Gara of Ireland holds the scoring record, with 557 points to Jonny Wilkinson's 546. O'Gara surpassed Wilkinson in the 2011 championship.

– O'Gara has also kicked the most penalties with 109 successful attempts.

– Brian O'Driscoll holds the record for the most Six Nation appearances, with sixty-five.

– Wales hold the record for fewest tries conceded in the Six Nations in one year. They conceded only two in their five matches in 2008.

– The 1977 Grand Slam-winning French team did not concede a single try in their four matches.

- Wales hold the record for the longest time without conceding a try, at just under six hours (358 minutes) in the 2013 tournament.

- The most points scored by a team in one match was 80, by England against Italy in 2001.

- England also scored the most ever points in a season, with 229 in 2001, as well as scoring the most tries in a season, in the same year, with twenty-nine.

- England's Jonny Wilkinson currently holds the record for individual points scored in one game. He notched up 35 points against Italy in 2001. He also scored the most points in one season, with 89 in 2001.

- Wilkinson also holds the most conversions record, with eighty-nine.

- The record number of tries scored in a match is held by George Lindsay of Scotland. He scored five tries against Wales in 1887.

- Ireland's Brian O'Driscoll holds the championship record for tries, having scored twenty-six in his Six Nations' career.

- England's Cyril Lowe and Scotland's Ian Smith share the record for the most tries in one season, with eight each (Lowe in 1914, Smith in 1925).

- In 1986 a team made up of representatives of the Five Nations played a one-off match against an Overseas Unions rugby union team. The game commemorated the centenary of the International Rugby Football Board. The game was played on Saturday 19 April. The Five Nations lost 32–13.

Players with the most overall appearances

65	Brian O'Driscoll (Ireland: 2000–2014)
63	Ronan O'Gara (Ireland: 2000–13)
56	Martin Castrogiovanni (Italy: 2002–15)
56	Mike Gibson (Ireland: 1964–79)
54	John Hayes (Ireland: 2000–10)
54	Jason Leonard (England: 1991–2004)
53	Willie John McBride (Ireland: 1962–75)
53	Chris Paterson (Scotland: 2000–11)
52	Gethin Jenkins (Wales: 2003–15)
51	Marco Bortolami (Italy: 2001–15)
51	Paul O'Connell (Ireland: 2002–15)
51	Martyn Williams (Wales: 1998–2010)
50	Stephen Jones (Wales: 1998–2011)
50	Sergio Parisse (Italy: 2004–15)
50	Philippe Sella (France: 1983–95)
50	Rory Underwood (England: 1984–96)
49	Andrea Lo Cicero (Italy: 2000–13)
49	Fabien Pelous (France: 1996–2006)
49	Fergus Slattery (Ireland: 1970–84)

Players who have scored the most points

557	Ronan O'Gara (Ireland: 2000–13)
546	Jonny Wilkinson (England: 1998–2011)
467	Stephen Jones (Wales: 1998–2011)
406	Neil Jenkins (Wales: 1991–2001)
403	Chris Paterson (Scotland: 2000–11)
288	Gavin Hastings (Scotland: 1986–95)
277	Leigh Halfpenny (Wales: 2009–15)
270	David Humphreys (Ireland: 1996–2005)
239	Johnny Sexton (Ireland: 2010–15)
232	Paul Grayson (England: 1996–2004)
217	Dimitri Yachvili (France: 2003–12)
207	Michael Kiernan (Ireland: 1982–91)

Players who have scored the most tries

26	Brian O'Driscoll (Ireland: 2000–14)
24	Ian Smith (Scotland: 1924–33)
22	Shane Williams (Wales: 2000–11)
18	Gareth Edwards (Wales: 1967–78)
18	C. N. Lowe (England: 1913–23)
18	Rory Underwood (England: 1984–96)
16	Ben Cohen (England: 2000–06)
16	Gerald Davies (Wales: 1967–78)
16	Kenny Jones (Wales: 1947–57)
16	Bill Llewellyn (Wales: 1899–1905)
15	Will Greenwood (England: 1998–2004)

15   J. L. Williams (Wales: 1907–11)

14   Serge Blanco (France: 1981–91)

14   Tommy Bowe (Ireland: 2006–15)

SIX NATIONS/FIVE NATIONS/ HOME NATIONS ROLL OF HONOUR

New Millennium: Six Nations

2015   Ireland

2014   Ireland

2013   Wales

2012   Wales (also Grand Slam winners)

2011   England

2010   France (also Grand Slam winners)

2009   Ireland (also Grand Slam winners)

2008   Wales (also Grand Slam winners)

2007   France (Ireland win Triple Crown)

2006   France (Ireland win Triple Crown)

2005   Wales (also Grand Slam winners)

2004   France (also Grand Slam winners; Ireland win Triple Crown)

2003   England (also Grand Slam winners)

2002   France (also Grand Slam winners; England win Triple Crown)

2001   England

2000   England

Recent Years: Five Nations

1999	Scotland
1998	France (also Grand Slam winners; England win Triple Crown)
1997	France (also Grand Slam winners; England win Triple Crown)
1996	England (also Triple Crown winners)
1995	England (also Grand Slam winners)
1994	Wales
1993	France
1992	England (also Grand Slam winners)
1991	England (also Grand Slam winners)
1990	Scotland (also Grand Slam winners)
1989	France
1988	Wales and France (Wales win Triple Crown)
1987	France (also Grand Slam winners)
1986	France and Scotland
1985	Ireland (also Triple Crown winners)
1984	Scotland (also Grand Slam winners)
1983	France and Ireland
1982	Ireland (also Triple Crown winners)
1981	France (also Grand Slam winners)
1980	England (also Grand Slam winners)

Post-war Years: Five Nations

1979	Wales (also Triple Crown winners)
1978	Wales (also Grand Slam winners)

1977	France (also Grand Slam winners; Wales win Triple Crown)
1976	Wales (also Grand Slam winners)
1975	Wales
1974	Ireland
1973	Five-way tie
1972	Not completed
1971	Wales (also Grand Slam winners)
1970	France and Wales
1969	Wales (also Triple Crown winners)
1968	France (also Grand Slam winners)
1967	France
1966	Wales
1965	Wales (also Triple Crown winners)
1964	Scotland and Wales
1963	England
1962	France
1961	France
1960	France and England (England win Triple Crown)
1959	France
1958	England
1957	England (also Grand Slam winners)
1956	Wales
1955	France and Wales
1954	England, France and Wales (England win Triple Crown)

1953   England

1952   Wales (also Grand Slam winners)

1951   Ireland

1950   Wales (also Grand Slam winners)

1949   Ireland (also Triple Crown winners)

1948   Ireland (also Grand Slam winners)

1947   Wales and England (France rejoins)

Interwar Years: Home and Five Nations

1939   England, Wales and Ireland

1938   Scotland (also Triple Crown winners)

1937   England (also Triple Crown winners)

1936   Wales

1935   Ireland

1934   England (also Triple Crown winners)

1933   Scotland (also Triple Crown winners)

1932   England, Wales and Ireland

1931   Wales

1930   England

1929   Scotland

1928   England (also Grand Slam winners)

1927   Scotland and Ireland

1926   Scotland and Ireland

1925   Scotland (also Grand Slam winners)

1924   England (also Grand Slam winners)

1923   England (also Grand Slam winners)

1922   Wales

1921   England (also Grand Slam winners)

1920   England, Scotland and Wales

Pre-war Years: Home and Five Nations

1914   England (also Grand Slam winners)

1913   England (also Grand Slam winners)

1912   England and Ireland

1911   Wales (also Grand Slam winners)

1910   England (France joins tournament)

1909   Wales (also Triple Crown winners)

1908   Wales (also Triple Crown winners)

1907   Scotland (also Triple Crown winners)

1906   Ireland and Wales

1905   Wales (also Triple Crown winners)

1904   Scotland

1903   Scotland (also Triple Crown winners)

1902   Wales (also Triple Crown winners)

1901   Scotland (also Triple Crown winners)

1900   Wales (also Triple Crown winners)

1899   Ireland (also Triple Crown winners)

1898   Not completed

1897   Not completed

1896   Ireland

1895   Scotland (also Triple Crown winners)

1894   Ireland (also Triple Crown winners)

1893   Wales (also Triple Crown winners)

1892   England (also Triple Crown winners)

1891   Scotland (also Triple Crown winners)

1890   England and Scotland

1889   Scotland

1888   Ireland, Scotland and Wales

1887   Scotland

1886   England and Scotland

1885   Not completed

1884   England (also Triple Crown winners)

1883   England (also Triple Crown winners)

1882   England (only England and Wales took part)

GRAND SLAM

–   In rugby union, a Grand Slam occurs when one team in the Six Nations Championship (or its Five Nations predecessor) beats all the others during that year's competition. This has been achieved thirty-seven times in total, the first time by Wales in 1908 and most recently in 2012, again by Wales.

–   The team that has won the most Grand Slams is England. They have won twelve in a period spanning ninety years (1913–2003).

–   There is no Grand Slam trophy. The term Grand Slam is used to recognise a championship-winning team, which has won all its games. The expression was first used in rugby in 1957, in a preview of a match between England and Scotland.

- A Grand Slam was not always available. It was contested during the periods 1908–31 and 1947–99 (Five Nations) and 2000–15 (Six Nations), a total of eighty-eight seasons to date. Grand Slams were won on thirty-seven of these occasions, by England (12), Wales (11), France (9), Scotland (3) and Ireland (2).

- Consecutive Grand Slams have been won by Wales in 1908 and 1909, by England in 1913 and 1914, 1923 and 1924, 1991 and 1992, and by France in 1997 and 1998. No team has ever won three consecutive Grand Slams.

Grand Slam Roll of Honour

England (12): 1913, 1914, 1921, 1923, 1924, 1928, 1957, 1980, 1991, 1992, 1995, 2003

Wales (11): 1908, 1909, 1911, 1950, 1952, 1971, 1976, 1978, 2005, 2008, 2012

France (9): 1968, 1977, 1981, 1987, 1997, 1998, 2002, 2004, 2010

Scotland (3): 1925, 1984, 1990

Ireland (2): 1948, 2009

Italy (0)

SIX NATIONS SCORING STATISTICS 2000–15

England: 2,218 points (232 tries)
France: 2,002 points (193 tries)

Ireland: 1,952 points (196 tries)

Wales: 1,834 points (166 tries)

Scotland: 1,256 points (91 tries)

Italy: 1,160 points (96 tries)

WOODEN SPOON

Italy (10): 2000, 2001, 2002, 2005, 2006, 2008, 2009, 2010, 2011, 2014

Scotland (4): 2004, 2007, 2012, 2015

Wales (1): 2003

France (1): 2013

England (0)

Ireland (0)

TRIPLE CROWN

- The Triple Crown is contested annually by the Home Nations, the four national teams of the British Isles who compete within the larger Six Nations Championship: England, Ireland, Scotland and Wales. If one team defeats all three other teams, they are awarded the Triple Crown.

- England were the first winners of the Triple Crown as it is known today, in the inaugural 1883 series of the Home Nations Championship.

- Originally there was no trophy. For the 2006 Six Nations, the Royal Bank of Scotland (the primary sponsor of the competition) commissioned Edinburgh and London-based Hamilton & Inches to design and create a new and permanent Triple Crown trophy. This has been awarded to Triple Crown-winning sides since 2006. Ireland was the first side to lift the trophy. It has been won three times by Ireland, twice by Wales and once by England.

– The first reference to the Triple Crown appeared in *Whitaker's Almanack 1900* (referring to the 1899 tournament).

– There has been a Triple Crown winner in sixty-four of the 118 competitions held from 1883 to 2014. (Twelve competitions were cancelled due to the two World Wars.)

– Two teams have won the Triple Crown in four successive years: Wales (1976–79) and England (1995–98). No other teams have won the Triple Crown more than twice in a row.

– Triple Crown winners who failed to go on to win the championship include Wales in 1977 and England in 1997, 1998, 2002 and 2014. Ireland, despite winning in 2004, 2006 and 2007, also failed to win the championship.

– Triple Crown winners who managed to share the championship are England in 1954 (lost to France, shared the title with Wales) and 1960 (drew with France and shared the title with them), and Wales in 1988 (lost to France and shared the title with them).

Triple Crown Roll of Honour

England (24): 1883, 1884, 1892, 1913, 1914, 1921, 1923, 1924, 1928, 1934, 1937, 1954, 1957, 1960, 1980, 1991, 1992, 1995, 1996, 1997, 1998, 2002, 2003, 2014

Wales (20): 1893, 1900, 1902, 1905, 1908, 1909, 1911, 1950, 1952, 1965, 1969, 1971, 1976, 1977, 1978, 1979, 1988, 2005, 2008, 2012

Ireland (10): 1894, 1899, 1948, 1949, 1982, 1985, 2004, 2006, 2007, 2009

Scotland (10): 1891, 1895, 1901, 1903, 1907, 1925, 1933, 1938, 1984, 1990

RBS SIX NATIONS MATCH-WINNING RATIO 2000–15

England:	55 wins	winning percentage: 68.8%
Ireland:	53 wins	winning percentage: 66.3%
France:	52 wins	winning percentage: 65.0%
Wales:	44 wins	winning percentage: 55.0%
Scotland:	19 wins	winning percentage: 23.8%
Italy:	12 wins	winning percentage: 15.0%

RUGBY IN THE SIX NATIONS COUNTRIES

IRELAND

–   Following the adoption of a set of official rules in 1868, rugby began to gain in popularity in Ireland. Early breeding grounds for rugby were Trinity College and St Columba's College. Fixtures were played as far back as 1867.

–   England played Ireland for the first time at The Oval in 1875. It was Ireland's first-ever Test match.

–   Ireland won their first championship in 1894, winning the Triple Crown also.

–   Ireland have won the Six Nations Championship and its precursors thirteen times outright and shared the title nine times.

–   When Irish internationals were played alternately in Belfast and Dublin, the UK national anthem was played before matches held in Belfast. 'Amhrán na bhFiann' ('The Soldiers' Song') was played for matches in Dublin. No anthem was played at away games.

–   In 1948 Jack Kyle inspired Ireland to beat France in Paris, England at Twickenham and Scotland at Lansdowne Road. The team then made history by winning a first Grand Slam in the Five Nations, with a win against the Welsh at Ravenhill, Belfast.

–   Ireland continued in a winning vein in 1949, winning the championship and Triple Crown.

–   On 27 February 1954 Ireland were due to play Scotland at Ravenhill in Belfast. Jim McCarthy, the team captain, told IRFU president Sarsfield Hogan that the eleven Republic-based players would not stand for 'God Save the Queen' alongside the Scottish team. An agreement was reached, and an abbreviated anthem, known in Ulster as 'The Salute' was played that afternoon. It was also agreed that the Irish team would never play again at Ravenhill. Ireland went on to beat Scotland 6–0. The Irish team did play in Northern Ireland again, in 2007.

–   The dawn of the professional rugby era began in dismal fashion for Ireland. They finished bottom in the Five Nations Championship three years in succession (1996, 1997 and 1998).

–   In March 2007 the IRFU formulated a new strategy called the High Performance Select Group. The group would contain up-and-coming Irish players who had the potential to break into future Irish teams. This group included players who would go on to become household names, including Luke Fitzgerald, Tommy Bowe, Rob Kearney, Stephen Ferris and Jamie Heaslip.

–   Ireland's strategy bore fruit when they won the 2009 Six Nations Championship and Grand Slam by beating Wales at the Millennium Stadium 15–17. It was the first time they had won the championship since 1985, and the first time they had won the Grand Slam since 1948.

– Ireland also became the second team (after Wales in 2005) to win a Six Nations Championship and the Grand Slam after playing more away fixtures than games at home.

– Four players have represented Ireland in 100 Tests or more: Brian O'Driscoll with 133 caps, Ronan O'Gara with 128, John Hayes with 105 and Paul O'Connell with 101.

– Brian O'Driscoll is Ireland's top try scorer, with forty-six. Denis Hickie (29), Tommy Bowe (28), Shane Horgan (21) and Girvan Dempsey (19) are next on the list.

– Ireland's youngest ever player was Frank Hewitt, who was aged seventeen years and 157 days when he lined out against Wales in 1924.

– The oldest player was John Hayes, who earned a cap against Scotland at the age of thirty-seven years and 277 days.

– On 10 June 2000 Ireland had their biggest ever Test match win. They defeated the USA in New Hampshire with an 80-point margin (83–3).

– Many politicians, from very different backgrounds, have played rugby for Ireland. These include Tyrone Howe (a former Unionist Party councillor), Trevor Ringland (an Ulster Unionist and Conservative parliamentary candidate) and Dick Spring (former Tánaiste and Labour Party leader).

- Former Irish President Éamon de Valera also played rugby and lined out for Rockwell College in a Munster Schools Senior Cup final.

- Ireland have never finished last in the Six Nations Championship.

Ireland Test Match Record (Tier 1 nations)

Opponent	Played	Won	Lost	Drew
Argentina	15	10	5	0
Australia	32	10	21	1
England	129	47	74	8
France	93	31	55	7
Italy	24	20	4	0
New Zealand	28	0	27	1
Scotland	130	59	66	5
South Africa	22	5	16	1
Wales	121	49	66	6

ENGLAND

- England's first international match was against Scotland on Monday 27 March 1871.

- They have won the Six Nations and its precursors on twenty-six occasions, which makes them the joint most successful team in the tournament's history. They have also won the Grand Slam twelve times.

- England defeated Scotland in 1880 to become

the first winners of the Calcutta Cup competition, which is now a regular part of the Six Nations fixture list.

–   Their longest wait between Championship wins is eighteen years (1892–1910).

–   England have been the most successful of the Home Nations in the Rugby World Cup, having won in 2003 and been runners-up in 1991 and 2007.

–   Four former England representatives have been inducted into the International Rugby Hall of Fame: Bill Beaumont, Martin Johnson, Jason Leonard and Wavell Wakefield.

–   The record for the most tries for England is held by Rory Underwood, with forty-nine.

–   The most capped England player is former prop Jason Leonard, who made 114 appearances over his fourteen-year career.

–   England's youngest ever Test player was Colin Laird, who was eighteen years and 134 days old when he played against Wales in 1927.

–   The youngest ever England captain was Will Carling. He represented England in seventy-two Tests.

–   Chris Oti's hat-trick of tries against Ireland in the 1988 championship is reputed to have inspired the selection of 'Swing Low, Sweet Chariot' as the English rugby team's anthem. A group of boys from a Benedictine school, following a tradition of their school games, sang the song after Oti's first try. When Oti scored his second try, amused spectators standing close to the boys joined in, and when Oti scored his hat-trick, the song rang out around the ground. Since then 'Swing Low, Sweet Chariot' has become England's spiritual anthem.

– The first-ever England coach was Don White, who was appointed on 20 December 1969.

– Interim coach Rob Andrew is the only English coach never to have won a match. He took the reins on 1 June 2008 for two losing Tests.

England Test Match Record (Tier 1 nations)

Opponent	Played	Won	Lost	Drew
Argentina	19	14	4	1
Australia	43	18	24	1
France	99	54	38	7
Ireland	129	74	47	8
Italy	21	21	0	0
New Zealand	40	7	32	1
Scotland	133	73	42	18
South Africa	37	12	23	2
Wales	126	58	56	12

SCOTLAND

- Scotland competed in the Five Nations from the inaugural tournament in 1883, winning it fourteen times outright.

- They won the last ever Five Nations Championship, in 1999. They have also shared the title on eight occasions.

- Since the beginning of the Six Nations Championship Scotland have not won the competition.

- The thistle is the national flower and also the symbol of the Scottish national rugby union team. According to legend the 'guardian thistle' played a part in the defence of Scotland against a night attack by Norwegian Vikings, one of whom let out a yell of pain when he stepped barefoot on a thistle, alerting the Scottish defenders.

- 'Flower of Scotland' has been used since 1990 as Scotland's unofficial national anthem. It was written by Roy Williamson of The Corries in 1967 and was adopted by the Scottish Rugby Union (SRU) to replace 'God Save the Queen'. Williamson wrote the song to have an energising effect on the squad as they contested the 1967 Five Nations Championship deciding match against England. Scotland went on to beat England 13–7 and win the Five Nations Championship with a Grand Slam.

- Scotland achieved 100 points for the first time when they defeated Japan 100–8 in November 2004. Their previous record had been 89–0 against Ivory Coast in the first round of the 1995 Rugby World Cup.

- On 21 November 2009 Scotland beat Australia. The narrow 9–8 win was their first after seventeen attempts in twenty-seven years.

- Ian Smith is the record try scorer, with twenty-four in his career.

- Chris Paterson, who spent most of his career with Edinburgh, has had the most appearances for Scotland, with 109.

- Chris Paterson also holds the points record, on 809.

Scotland Test Match Record (Tier 1 nations)

Opponent	Played	Won	Lost	Drew
Argentina	15	6	9	0
Australia	28	9	19	0
England	133	42	73	18
France	88	34	51	3
Ireland	130	66	59	5
Italy	23	15	8	0
New Zealand	30	0	28	2
South Africa	25	5	20	0
Wales	120	48	69	3

WALES

- Welsh Rugby Union (WRU) was established in 1881. Wales played their first international against England that year.

- In 1905 Wales faced New Zealand's All Blacks at Cardiff Arms Park. Up to that point New Zealand (the Originals) were undefeated on their tour of the British Isles. Having defeated England, Ireland and Scotland, they lost to Wales. It was New Zealand's only defeat in their thirty-five-match tour.

- Wales have won the Six Nations Championship and its precursors twenty-six times outright, joint first with England.

- Wales was the dominant force in the Six Nations competition between 1969 and 1980. They won on eight occasions, including three shared wins.

- Neil Jenkins of Wales was the first rugby player to surpass 1,000 Test points. Jenkins scored 1,049 points for Wales and he kicked 235 successful penalties. He also holds the record for most points in a single Test match, with 30.

- The record for drop goals for Wales is held by Jonathan Davies, with thirteen.

- Shane Williams is Wales' record try scorer, with fifty-eight tries. He is also Wales' record try scorer in Six Nations Championships, with twenty-two, and in the Rugby World Cup, with ten.

– Colin Charvis' total of twenty-two tries means he holds the Welsh record for a forward. This was also the highest number scored by a forward in world rugby until 2011.

– Gethin Jenkins is the nation's most capped player, with 114 Welsh caps.

– Three other Welsh players to have earned 100 caps or more are Stephen Jones, with 104, and Gareth Thomas and Martyn Williams, with 100 each.

– The record for most Tests as captain is held by Ryan Jones, with thirty-three.

– The record for the most consecutive appearances is held by Gareth Edwards who played all fifty-three of his Tests for Wales consecutively between 1967 and 1978. Edwards was also Wales' youngest ever captain, at the age of twenty.

– The youngest player capped for Wales is Tom Prydie. He made his debut for Wales in the 2010 Six Nations, against Italy. He was aged eighteen years and twenty-five days. This beat the mark set by Norman Biggs in 1888.

– Paul Thorburn of Wales holds the world record for the longest successful kick in an international Test match. He secured the record during the 1986 Five Nations Championship, at Cardiff Arms Park. The penalty kick measured exactly 70 yards 8½ inches (64.2 metres) against Scotland.

Wales Test Match Record (Tier 1 nations)

Opponent	Played	Won	Lost	Drew
Argentina	15	10	5	0
Australia	38	10	27	1
England	126	56	58	12
France	93	47	43	3
Ireland	121	66	49	6
Italy	22	19	2	1
New Zealand	30	3	27	0
Scotland	120	69	48	3
South Africa	30	2	27	1

ITALY

–   The first match played by a representative Italian XV took place in 1911, between Milan and Voiron of France.

–   In May 1929 Italy played their first international, losing 9–0 to Spain in Barcelona.

–   There are just over 1,000 rugby clubs in Italy. They are mainly centred in the rugby heartlands of Veneto and Lombardy.

–   Since 2000 Italy have competed annually in the Six Nations Championship. They made a historic winning start by defeating Scotland in their first-ever match.

–   Italy have been the holders of the Giuseppe Garibaldi Trophy, which is awarded each year to the winners of the Six Nations match between France and Italy, just once, in 2013.

– Marcello Cuttitta is their record try scorer, with twenty-five.

– Diego Dominguez has scored the most points, with 983, of which nine were tries.

– The oldest player on an Italian national team was prop forward Sergio Lanfranchi, aged thirty-eight years and 184 days.

– The youngest ever Italian player was Pietro Vinci, aged sixteen years and 176 days when he took to the field against Spain on 20 May 1929.

– Italy used to play their home games at the Stadio Flaminio, Rome. The stadium had a capacity of just under 25,000. They moved to the larger Stadio Olimpico in 2011.

– Italy competed in the original European championships from 1936–38, but the Second World War spelled the end of that tournament. Italy competed in all the European tournaments organised by FIRA – the European Cup, the Nations Cup and the FIRA trophy – from 1952–1997, until they became part of the Six Nations.

– Italy achieved only one victory in the Fédération Internationale de Rugby Amateur Trophy, in its last outing of 1995–97.

Italy Test Match Record (Tier 1 nations)

Opponent	Played	Won	Lost	Drew
Argentina	20	5	14	1
Australia	16	0	16	0
England	21	0	21	0
France	36	3	33	0
Ireland	24	4	20	0
New Zealand	12	0	12	0
Scotland	23	8	15	0
South Africa	12	0	12	0
Wales	22	2	19	1

FRANCE

– Rugby was introduced to France in 1872 by British expats.

– On New Year's Day 1906 the national team played its first Test match, against the New Zealand All Blacks in Paris.

– Until 1912 the strip of the French team was white with two rings, one red and one blue.

– France joined the Home Nations to form the Five Nations tournament in 1910.

– When France won against Scotland in 1911, France's captain Marcel Communeau called for the team to adopt the *coq gaulois* (Gallic rooster), a historical symbol of France, as its emblem.

- France have won the Five/Six Nations sixteen times and shared it a further eight times. They have also won a total of nine Grand Slams.

- They won their first Five Nations Championship outright in 1959. It was not until 1968 that they won their first Grand Slam.

- France were ejected from the Five Nations in 1932. They were deemed to be paying players, which was considered an act of professionalism under the competition's rules.

- France also competed in the rugby competitions at the early Summer Olympics, winning the gold medal in 1900 and two silver medals in the 1920s.

- France reached the first Rugby World Cup Final and lost to New Zealand. They have reached the final on two other occasions, losing to New Zealand again in 2011 and Australia in 1999.

- France have hosted the World Cup twice, in 1991 (jointly with Great Britain) and 2007. On both occasions they were beaten in the tournament by England.

- France are the third-highest World Cup point scorers of all time, with 1,195 points. They are also the third-highest try scorers and the second-highest penalty scorers. France's Thierry Lacroix was the top scorer in the 1995 tournament, with 112 points.

- Former French great Jean-Pierre Rives won fifty-nine Tests for France between 1975 and 1984. The former French captain, who is now a sculptor, designed the Giuseppe Garibaldi Trophy. The trophy, now an annual part of the Six Nations calendar, is contested between France and Italy.

France Test Match Record (Tier 1 nations)

Opponent	Played	Won	Lost	Drew
Argentina	48	34	13	1
Australia	46	18	26	2
England	99	38	54	7
Ireland	94	56	31	7
Italy	36	33	3	0
New Zealand	55	12	42	1
Scotland	88	51	34	3
South Africa	39	11	22	6
Wales	95	44	48	3

SOUTHERN HEMISPHERE RUGBY

NEW ZEALAND

–   New Zealand are the leading Test match point scorers in rugby history. The All Blacks have won over three-quarters of all Test matches they have played (76 per cent). They hold a winning record against every country they have played since their international debut in 1903.

–   Ireland have played New Zealand twenty-eight times and have not recorded a victory.

–   Only five nations – South Africa, England, France, Australia and Wales – have ever defeated New Zealand in Test matches.

–   France, Ireland, Argentina, Fiji, Samoa, Tonga, Japan and Portugal have all suffered their worst defeat at the hands of New Zealand.

–   The team's first match was in 1884 against Cumberland County, New South Wales. Their first international match was against Australia, in Sydney in 1903.

–   The following year they hosted their first-ever home Test, a match against a British Isles side, in Wellington. This was followed by a tour of Europe and North America. There they suffered their first-ever Test defeat, to Wales in Cardiff, in 1905.

- New Zealand have held number one ranking longer than all the other teams combined, since the introduction of the IRB's world rankings in October 2003.

- New Zealand compete with Argentina, Australia and South Africa in the Rugby Championship, which was known as the Tri Nations before Argentina's entry in 2012.

- The All Blacks have won the trophy thirteen times in the competition's nineteen-year history.

- New Zealand have achieved a Grand Slam (defeating England, Ireland, Scotland and Wales in one tour) on four occasions (1978, 2005, 2008 and 2010).

- They have also been named the IRB Team of the Year eight times since the introduction of the award in 2001.

- New Zealand jointly hosted (with Australia) and won the first Rugby World Cup. They defeated France 29–9 in the final at Eden Park, Auckland. New Zealand conceded only 52 points in the entire tournament. They scored forty-three tries in six games en route to winning the title, beating Italy, Fiji, Argentina, Scotland, Wales and France.

- The All Blacks' greatest Test win was 145–17 against Japan in 1995. Their greatest loss was a 28–7 loss to Australia in 1999.

- New Zealand hold several World Cup records, including most World Cup matches played (43). They have also accumulated most points over all the World Cups (2,012), most tries overall (272) and most conversions (198).

- The All Blacks have never lost a World Cup match in the pool stages. In fact they have topped their pool in all seven Rugby World Cups.

- The All Blacks' record Test try scorer is Doug Howlett, with forty-nine tries. He overtook Christian Cullen (forty-six) during the 2007 World Cup.

- The world record for tries in a calendar year is held by Joe Rokocoko, who scored seventeen tries in 2003.

- Rokocoko also became the first All Black to score ten tries in his first five Tests and the first All Black to score at least two tries in each of four consecutive Test matches.

- The most capped All Black is Richie McCaw, with 137 caps.

- The youngest All Black to play in a Test match was Jonah Lomu, capped at age nineteen years and forty-five days.

- The oldest Test player was Ned Hughes, at forty years and 123 days.

- Dan Carter holds the record for points against Australia, with 270.

- There have been seventeen sets of father and son All Blacks and thirty-two sets of brothers.

All Blacks Test Match Record (Tier 1 nations)

Opponents	Played	Won	Lost	Drew
Argentina	20	19	0	1
Australia	152	104	41	7
British & Irish Lions	38	29	6	3
England	40	32	7	1
France	55	42	12	1
Ireland	28	27	0	1
Italy	12	12	0	0
Scotland	30	28	0	2
South Africa	89	51	35	3
Wales	30	27	3	0

AUSTRALIA

- Rugby union has a long history in Australia, with the first club being formed in 1864 at Sydney University.

- The first reports of a sport like rugby being played in Australia date back to the 1820s, when visiting ship crews would play army teams at Barrack Square, Perth.

- The first meeting of the Australian Rugby Football Union was held on 25 November 1949. There were eleven delegates present from New South

Wales, Queensland, South Australia, Western Australia, Tasmania and Victoria.

– The Australian Capital Territory became a member in 1972 and the Northern Territory became an associate member in 1978.

– In 1903 Australia played their first Test against the All Blacks in front of a crowd of 30,000 at the Sydney Cricket Ground.

– The first international tour was organised for 1908, when a squad of players spent nine months travelling in the United Kingdom, Ireland and North America. The team was invited to play in the rugby tournament of the 1908 London Olympic Games and they won the gold medal, defeating the English team.

– The Wallabies have won the Rugby World Cup twice, in 1991 and 1999.

– They have won the Tri Nations competition three times in sixteen years, in 2000, 2001 and 2011.

– The Wallabies have played in Australia's traditional sporting colours of green and gold since 1929.

– Australia and New Zealand compete for the Bledisloe Cup. Australia have won the cup just twelve times since 1932.

– In 1984 Australia toured the UK and Ireland with a young side and a new coach, Alan Jones. The 1984 Wallabies made history when they became the first team from Australia to achieve a Grand Slam by defeating all four Home Nations – England, Ireland, Wales and Scotland – as well as a strong Barbarians side.

- Australia has a large player base, with 82,000 players nationwide.

- Michael Lynagh is the Australian's record points scorer, with 911.

- Mat Rogers scored the most points in a single game, with 42 against Namibia.

- As well as making a record 139 appearances for the Wallabies, George Gregan was also the most capped captain, with fifty-nine appearances in this role.

Australia Test Match Record (Tier 1 nations)

Opponent	Played	Won	Lost	Drew
Argentina	23	17	5	1
British & Irish Lions	23	6	17	0
England	43	24	18	1
France	46	26	18	2
Ireland	32	21	10	1
Italy	16	16	0	0
New Zealand	152	41	104	7
Scotland	28	19	9	0
South Africa	80	34	45	1
Wales	38	27	10	1

SOUTH AFRICA

–   The South African national rugby union team are generally known as the Springboks.

–   The Springboks play in green and gold jerseys with white shorts, and their emblems are the springbok and the protea.

–   The Springboks played their first-ever Test match on 30 July 1891, against a British Isles touring team. This first South African international took place at Port Elizabeth's St George's Park Cricket Ground.

–   South Africa does not have a designated home stadium, but plays in various locations around the country.

–   Ellis Park Stadium was built in 1928, and in 1955 it hosted a record 100,000 people for a Test between South Africa and the British and Irish Lions.

–   The Springboks made their World Rugby Cup debut in 1995, when they hosted the tournament. They defeated the All Blacks 15–12 in the final.

–   South Africa regained their title as champions twelve years later, when they defeated England 15–6 in the 2007 final.

–   South Africa has competed in the annual Rugby Championship (formerly the Tri Nations) with Australia and New Zealand since 1996. South

Africa has won the competition on three occasions, in 1998, 2004 and 2009.

– South Africa also participates in the Mandela Challenge Plate with Australia and the Freedom Cup with New Zealand as part of the Rugby Championship.

– Victor Matfield is the most capped lock in rugby history, with all of his 121 caps being gained in that position. While Fabien Pelous of France retired with 118 caps, only 100 were as a lock.

– Percy Montgomery holds the South African record for Test points, with 893. At the time of his international retirement that placed him sixth on the all-time list of Test point scorers. He is now in ninth position. The most points Montgomery ever scored in a single international was 35, against Namibia in 2007. This is also a South African record.

– Fly-half Jannie de Beer holds the world record for drop goals in a Test match. He scored five during the 44–21 quarter-final win over England in the 1999 Rugby World Cup.

– In 2009 John Smit became the world's most capped captain, having captained South Africa in eighty-two of his 111 Tests. He has since been overtaken by Richie McCaw and Brian O'Driscoll.

– Smit played forty-six consecutive matches for South Africa, a record.

- Smit retired in 2011 as the most capped Springbok of all time with 111. At the time, this placed him joint-sixth (with Philippe Sella of France) on the all time list of most capped international players.

- On 1 August 2009, during the Tri Nations tournament, Morné Steyn set a number of records in the second Test between the Springboks and the All Blacks. The Springboks won 31–19, with Steyn scoring all South Africa's points – one try, one conversion and eight penalties. Steyn's haul of records included:

  > the most points scored by any player in a Tri Nations match, surpassing Andrew Mehrtens (All Blacks v Australia, 1999)

  > the most points ever scored by a player in a Test against the All Blacks, overtaking the mark set by Christophe Lamaison of France in 1999 (27)

  > the world record for the most points scored by a player who has scored all their team's points in a match

  > the South African record for penalties in a Test (8), beating the seven achieved twice by Percy Montgomery.

- South Africa also has the world's most capped lock pairing of Victor Matfield and Bakkies Botha, who have started together in sixty-two Tests.

– The record try scorer for the Springboks is Bryan Habana, with fifty-seven tries.

South Africa Test Match Record (Tier 1 nations)

Opponent	Played	Won	Lost	Drew
Argentina	19	18	0	1
Australia	80	45	34	1
British & Irish Lions	46	23	17	6
England	37	23	12	2
France	39	22	11	6
Ireland	22	16	5	1
Italy	12	12	0	0
New Zealand	89	35	51	3
Scotland	25	20	5	0
Wales	30	27	2	1

ARGENTINA

– The team's emblem is a jaguar, but they are known as the Pumas. The nickname came from the team's tour of Rhodesia in 1965. A local journalist dubbed the touring side the Pumas because the team's emblem bore more resemblance to a puma than a jaguar.

– Argentina made their international Test debut, in 1910, against a touring British Isles team. The Pumas lost 28–3.

– Argentina competed at the first-ever Rugby World

Cup, held in Australia and New Zealand, in 1987. They finished bottom of their pool after being defeated by the All Blacks and Fiji.

– In 1999 Argentina finished in a three-way tie in their pool with Wales and Samoa, but third on points scored. They made it through the knockout stage but were beaten in the quarter-finals by the French 47–26 in a high-scoring encounter. Despite the defeat, fly-half Gonzalo Quesada was the tournament's top scorer. The man from Buenos Aires scored 102 points.

– Famous players include Hugo Porta, a member of both the International Rugby and IRB Halls of Fame, who played during the 1970s and 1980s, and past Pumas captain Agustín Pichot.

– Former captain Felipe Contepomi and his team-mate Juan Martín Hernández both made the five-man shortlist for the IRB International Player of the Year award in 2007.

– Former player Marcelo Loffreda coached the Pumas to third place in the 2007 Rugby World Cup, before leaving to take up the head coaching job at English club Leicester Tigers.

– Felipe Contepomi is Argentina's most capped player, with eighty-seven caps to his name.

– Winger José Núñez Piossek is the try-scoring record holder, with more tries (29) than games played (28).

– Contepomi, with 651 points in eighty-seven starts, is the top points scorer.

– Centre Lisandro Arbizu won the most caps as captain, with forty-eight.

Argentina Test Match Record (Tier 1 nations)

Opponent	Played	Won	Lost	Drew
Australia	23	5	17	1
British & Irish Lions	7	0	6	1
England	20	4	14	2
France	48	13	34	1
Ireland	20	7	12	1
Italy	20	14	5	1
New Zealand	24	0	23	1
Scotland	18	10	8	0
South Africa	19	0	18	1
Wales	18	6	11	1

THE BLEDISLOE CUP

– Rugby union's Bledisloe Cup is contested by Australia and New Zealand.

– The outright winner is decided over the course of three Tests, which includes the Rugby Championship.

– Bledisloe Cup matches count as part of the Rugby Championship (formerly the Tri Nations).

- It is named after Lord Bledisloe, the former Governor-General of New Zealand, who donated the trophy in 1931.

- The trophy, crafted by Walker & Hall in Sheffield, is the largest trophy in world rugby.

- The trophy, which was once contested every few years, is now an annual event.

- 2008 saw a Bledisloe Cup match held outside both countries for the first time, when the teams met in Hong Kong.

- The Bledisloe Cup has also been contested in Tokyo, when a match was played there on 31 October 2009.

- New Zealand has dominated the cup, winning it twelve times in a row (2003–14).

- Most titles have been won by New Zealand (42).

- Australia has won the competition on twelve occasions.

- Australia won the competition five times in a row between 1998 and 2002.

THE RUGBY CHAMPIONSHIP (FORMERLY TRI NATIONS)

- The Rugby Championship is contested annually by Argentina, Australia, New Zealand and South Africa.

- Prior to the 2012 tournament, when Argentina joined, it was known as the Tri Nations. The competition was first played in 1996, when New Zealand became champions having won all of their matches.

- New Zealand also won the first-ever Rugby Championship in 2012, winning all of their six fixtures.

- The competition is administered by SANZAR, a three-nation consortium formed by the Southern Hemisphere's big three international bodies: the Australian, New Zealand and South African Rugby Unions.

- Bryan Habana of South Africa is the top try scorer in the competition, with eighteen.

- The competition's top points scorer is Dan Carter of New Zealand, with 531 points.

- The highest attendance at a Rugby Championship match was 88,739 for New Zealand v South Africa in 2012.

- In the eighteen Rugby Championship matches played so far, New Zealand has won sixteen, drawn one and lost one (to South Africa in 2014).

IRISH RUGBY LEGENDS

BRIAN O'DRISCOLL

- O'Driscoll was born on 21 January 1979 in Clontarf, Dublin.

- The O'Driscoll family are steeped in rugby. Brian's father, Frank, played twice for Ireland (non-Test matches). His uncle Barry also won four caps. Another uncle, John, was an accomplished Irish international. He won twenty-six Irish caps and was a member of the British and Irish Lions touring side in 1980 and 1983.

- Brian's first love was Gaelic football, which he played as a young boy.

- He went to school in Blackrock College and was an integral part of the Senior Cup team in 1996 and 1997. He was elevated to school's captain in 1997. The side reached the quarter-final but were defeated by a strong Clongowes outfit, who boasted a certain Gordon D'Arcy in their side.

- In 1996 he represented the Ireland Schools team on three occasions.

- O'Driscoll played for Ireland before he played for the senior Leinster team.

- O'Driscoll made his debut for Leinster in August

1999, against Munster. Aussie Matt Williams was the head coach.

- In April 1999 O'Driscoll was part of the Ireland squad that played a friendly against Italy.

- He won his first Test cap on 12 June 1999. Aged twenty, he took to the field in Brisbane as part of the tour of Australia. Ireland suffered a 46–10 loss to Australia.

- In 2000 O'Driscoll made his mark on the international stage. A hat-trick of tries in a Six Nations Championship victory against France in Paris led Ireland to a famous victory over Les Bleus. It was Ireland's first win in Paris since 1972.

- In 2002 O'Driscoll was given the captain's armband for the first time. Ireland won 18–9 against Australia in their first win over the side since 1979.

- O'Driscoll's popularity in Ireland was reflected in a new line of T-shirts. They bore the slogan 'In BOD We Trust'.

- In 2003, when Irish legend Keith Wood called it a day, O'Driscoll was awarded the captaincy on a permanent basis.

- O'Driscoll was controversially injured for the Lions in the early stages of the first Test against the All Blacks, in Christchurch on 25 June 2005. The infamous 'spear tackle' by All Blacks skipper

Tana Umaga and Keven Mealamu cast a long shadow over the tour. The Irishman suffered a dislocated shoulder.

– On 30 April 2013 O'Driscoll got the call to play in his fourth British and Irish Lions tour. He was only the third player in the 125-year history of the tour to do so.

– O'Driscoll appeared three times for the invitational Barbarians rugby team (the Baa-Baas). He scored his first and only try for them against South Africa on 10 December 2000.

– O'Driscoll was nominated for the prestigious IRB World Player of the Year in 2001, 2002 and 2009.

– O'Driscoll was Player of the Tournament in three RBS Six Nations Championships (2006, 2007 and 2009).

Honours

Leinster

Celtic League (4): 2002, 2008, 2013, 2014
Heineken Cup (3): 2009, 2011, 2012
Amlin Challenge Cup (1): 2013

Ireland

Under-19 Rugby World Championship (1): 1998
Six Nations Championship (2): 2009, 2014
Grand Slam (1): 2009

Triple Crown (4): 2004, 2006, 2007, 2009

British and Irish Lions tours (4): 2001, 2005 (captain), 2009, 2013 (series victory)

PAUL O'CONNELL

- O'Connell made his debut for Ireland against Wales in the 2002 Six Nations Championship, starting alongside Mick Galwey and scoring a try.

- He was chosen for the Ireland squad for the 2003 Rugby World Cup and played against Romania, Namibia, Argentina and Australia in the pool stage, and in the 43–21 quarter-final defeat to France.

- In Ireland's opening game of the 2004 Six Nations Championship, O'Connell captained the side in the absence of Brian O'Driscoll.

- He was part of the team that overcame Scotland on 27 March 2004, securing Ireland's first Triple Crown since 1985. He was also part of the Ireland teams that won Triple Crowns in 2006 and 2007, and the Grand Slam in 2009.

- O'Connell scored the last ever international try at the old Lansdowne Road before it was demolished and rebuilt as the Aviva Stadium. It capped a memorable day for the man from Limerick, as Ireland beat the Pacific Islanders 61–17.

- O'Connell was shortlisted for the International Rugby Board Player of the Year in 2006 and was the only northern hemisphere nominee. The other four nominees were Dan Carter, Richie McCaw, Chris Latham and Fourie du Preez. McCaw was the eventual winner.

- O'Connell again took over from an injured O'Driscoll as Ireland captain in their historic match against France in the 2007 Six Nations Championship, the first rugby match ever played at Croke Park.

- O'Connell was awarded the man-of-the-match accolade following Ireland's historic (and record-breaking) 43–13 win over England at Croke Park during the 2007 Six Nations Championship.

- O'Connell made his debut for Munster on 17 August 2001, in a Celtic League fixture against Edinburgh.

- He started for Munster in their Heineken Cup Final defeat to Leicester Tigers on 25 May 2002.

- He was part of the Munster squad that won the 2002–03 Celtic League.

- O'Connell also won the 2005 Celtic Cup with Munster, defeating Llanelli Scarlets 27–16 in the final.

- O'Connell was an integral member of the Munster team that won the 2006 Heineken Cup, playing a

- crucial role in defeating Biarritz Olympique 19–23 in the final.
- He became Munster captain in July 2007, succeeding Anthony Foley.
- O'Connell led Munster to their second Heineken Cup triumph in the 2008 season, defeating Toulouse 16–13.
- He also led the side to victory in the 2009 Celtic League.
- O'Connell was selected in the squad for the 2005 British and Irish Lions tour to New Zealand. He won his first Test cap for the Lions on 25 June 2005, starting in the first Test defeat to New Zealand.
- In April 2009 O'Connell was named as the British and Irish Lions captain for that year's tour to South Africa.
- O'Connell was selected for his third Lions tour on 30 April 2013.

Honours

Munster

Heineken Cup (2): 2006, 2008
Celtic League (3): 2003, 2009, 2011
Celtic Cup (1): 2005

Ireland

Six Nations Championship (3): 2009, 2014, 2015

Grand Slam (1): 2009

Triple Crown (4): 2004, 2006, 2007, 2009

British and Irish Lions tours (3): 2005, 2009 (captain), 2013

WILLIE JOHN McBRIDE

- McBride was born in Toomebridge, County Antrim, on 6 June 1940.

- He was a latecomer to the game and began playing rugby at the age of seventeen.

- He joined Ballymena RFC and in 1962 was selected to play for Ireland.

- His first Test, on 10 February 1962, was against England at Twickenham.

- He was a member of the Irish team that defeated South Africa in 1965, and when Ireland became the first Home Nations team to defeat a major southern-hemisphere team (Australia) in their own country, he played a starring role.

- McBride was appointed captain of the 1974 Lions tour to South Africa. The Lions won the Test series 3–0, the first time they won a series in South Africa.

- In 1975 he played his last game at Lansdowne Road. The game was against France. In a fairytale ending McBride crossed the line for his first-ever Irish try.

- He pulled on the green jersey for the last time against Wales in Cardiff on Saturday 15 March 1975.

- He won sixty-three international caps for Ireland, including eleven as skipper.

- He toured with the Lions five times – a record that gave him seventeen Lions Test caps – and was manager of the 1983 Lions tour to New Zealand.

- He was awarded an MBE for his services to the game of rugby in 1971.

- McBride coached the Irish team from 1983–84.

- In 1997 he was one of the first inductees into the International Rugby Hall of Fame.

- In 2004 he was named by *Rugby World* magazine as Heineken Rugby Personality of the Century.

Honours

Five Nations Championship (2): 1973, 1974

British and Irish Lions (5): 1962, 1966, 1968, 1971, 1974

JACK KYLE

- Jack Kyle was born on 10 January 1926 in Belfast, Northern Ireland.

- He was voted the greatest-ever Irish player in an IRFU poll in 2002.

- Kyle had several nicknames, including Ghost and the Scarlet Pimpernel.

- He began playing rugby at school, at the Belfast Royal Academy.

- Kyle was a one-club man, spending his entire career with Queen's University RFC, Belfast.

- He played his first match for Ireland during the Second World War, a friendly against a British Army XV. No caps were awarded for the fixture.

- He played for Ireland forty-six times and, amazingly, scored 46 points! The scores included seven tries and one drop goal.

- He made his international debut on 25 January 1947 against the French. His last appearance for Ireland was on 1 March 1958 against Scotland.

- In his final outing for Ireland against Scotland, he became the most capped player in international rugby, with fifty-two. These included six Lions Tests. It meant he overtook the previous mark set by Jean Prat of France, who had retired in 1955 with fifty-one caps.

- Kyle featured in every post-war international for Ireland until he was selected for the British and Irish Lions in 1950.

- His first Lions match was against provincial side Buller in 1950. His first Test was against New Zealand. The last time he donned the Lions jersey was on 18 September 1950 against Ceylon (now Sri Lanka) in a non-cap international.

- He played for the Lions in twenty tour matches including six Tests (four against New Zealand and two against Australia).

- His Five Nations Championship record is twenty-two won, sixteen lost and four draws.

- He was international captain on six occasions (won two, lost three, drew one).

- Kyle played in every Five Nations tournament between 1947 and 1958.

- He became the first fly-half to win fifty caps, against Australia in 1958.

- He also lined out for and skippered the Barbarians.

- He played in one Services International for Ireland against the British Army in 1945 in Belfast and in two Victory Internationals in 1946, against France and England.

- He played for Ulster against the Kiwis in 1945, Australia in 1947 and South Africa in 1951.

- Jack Kyle died at his home in Bryansford, Northern Ireland, on 27 November 2014, after a long illness.

Honours

Five Nations Championship (3): 1948, 1949, 1951
Grand Slam (1): 1948
Triple Crown (2): 1948, 1949
British and Irish Lions tours (1): 1950

RONAN O'GARA

- Ronan O'Gara was born on 7 March 1977 in San Diego, California, USA.

- He is Ireland's second most capped player of all time (128), behind Brian O'Driscoll, and the fourth most capped in rugby union history.

- O'Gara played his first senior match for Ireland in an A International against Italy on 9 April 1999.

- He wore the green jersey at full international level for the first time against Scotland on 19 February 2000, during the Six Nations Championship.

- He is Ireland's all-time highest points scorer. He is also the fourth-highest points scorer in the history of international rugby union.

- O'Gara has scored more tries (16) for Ireland than any other fly-half in history.

- He also holds the Munster all-time points record, with 2,625, and the Heineken Cup record for points scored, with 1,365.

- O'Gara and David Wallace, both of whom would go on to become Munster legends, made their debuts together against Connacht in August 1997. O'Gara scored 19 points.

- O'Gara made his Heineken Cup debut against London Harlequins in September 1997 in the 1997–98 Heineken Cup. He scored 15 points with the boot, but Munster lost the game 48–40.

- O'Gara was assured of a place in Munster folklore when his last-minute conversion against Gloucester on 18 January 2003 helped Munster to a 27-point victory, which took them through to the Heineken Cup quarter-final. The game would be forever remembered in Munster as 'the Miracle Match'.

- O'Gara turned down the chance to join NFL side Miami Dolphins in March 2003.

- O'Gara kicked five points for Munster in their 16–10 Heineken Cup semi-final defeat to Clermont Auvergne on 27 April 2013, in what was his last game for his beloved Munster. He announced his retirement on 18 May 2013, after weeks of speculation.

Honours

Munster

Heineken Cup (2): 2006, 2008

Celtic League (3): 2003, 2009, 2011

Celtic Cup (1): 2004–05

Irish Interprovincial Championship (3): 1999, 2000, 2001

Ireland

Six Nations Championship (1): 2009

Grand Slam (1): 2009

Triple Crown (4): 2004, 2006, 2007, 2009

British and Irish Lions tours (3): 2001, 2005, 2009

MIKE GIBSON

- Michael Henderson Gibson MBE was born on 3 December 1942 in Belfast.

- Gibson's Irish rugby career began in 1964 and he went on to represent his country in four different positions.

- His career spanned fifteen years at international level, during which he appeared in eighty-one Tests.

- Gibson toured with the British and Irish Lions five times. In 1977 he was selected as one of the backs to go on the tour to New Zealand. This was his fifth Lions tour, a record only equalled by Willie John McBride. However, injuries limited his participation and he was unable to compete for a Test place.

– He was thirty-six when he gained his sixty-ninth and final Irish cap, in the second Test match against their hosts during Ireland's 1979 tour of Australia.

– Gibson scored 112 Test points (nine tries, sixteen penalties, seven conversions and six drop goals) for Ireland.

– Gibson's Ireland caps haul of sixty-nine was beaten by lock Malcolm O'Kelly against Scotland in February 2005. His record had lasted for twenty-six years.

– His record of fifty-six appearances in the Five Nations was first equalled by Ronan O'Gara in Ireland's final match of the 2011 Six Nations.

– For the majority of his career Gibson played for North of Ireland FC. While studying law at Cambridge, he also played for the university's team.

– He continued playing club rugby until the age of forty-two.

– Since retirement Gibson has worked as a solicitor in Belfast. Fellow Irish international David Humphreys trained as a solicitor at Gibson's firm.

- Gibson was one of the first inductees into the International Rugby Hall of Fame and in 2010 was also an inductee to the International Rugby Board (World Rugby) Hall of Fame.

Honours

Five Nations Championship (2): 1973, 1974

British and Irish Lions tours (5): 1966, 1968, 1971, 1974, 1977

WORLD RUGBY LEGENDS

DAN CARTER (New Zealand)

–   Daniel William Carter was born on 5 March 1982 in Southbridge, Canterbury, New Zealand.

–   He has been named the International Rugby Board Player of the Year twice, in 2005 and 2012.

–   His great-uncle was Canterbury and New Zealand legend Bill Dalley, a member of the 1924–25 Invincibles.

–   Carter made his provincial debut for Canterbury in 2002 and the following season was signed by the Crusaders.

–   In June 2003 Carter played his first match for the All Blacks, aged twenty-one, in Hamilton, New Zealand. In the match he scored 20 points in New Zealand's decisive win over Wales.

–   In 2005 Carter gave a man-of-the-match performance in the All Blacks 48–18 win over the British and Irish Lions. He kicked five penalties and four conversions, and also scored two tries. His total of 33 points set a new All Blacks record, overtaking the previous mark of 18 points in a Lions Test.

–   In April 2008 Carter was linked with several European clubs, including Toulouse. They offered

Carter one of the biggest contracts in rugby history, at £750,000 per annum. Carter decided against the massive contract and instead chose another French Top 14 club side, USA Perpignan.

– When he scored a penalty from the halfway line against Wales in November 2007, Carter became the highest points scorer of all time. With that penalty he overtook Jonny Wilkinson's record of 1,178.

– Wilkinson regained the record on 26 February 2011 in England's Six Nations match against the French. His new record stood for just five months, when Carter set a new mark of 1,204 points in the first Tri Nations match of the 2011 series, against South Africa.

– Carter is currently the highest point scorer in Test match rugby, with 1,455 points.

– After being vice-captain for more than fifty Tests under Richie McCaw, Carter was promoted to captain, but an injury prevented him from actually captaining the side.

– On 16 November 2013 Carter became the fifth All Black to reach 100 caps for his country, in a match that saw New Zealand defeat England 30–22 at Twickenham.

– Carter was part of the Tri Nations/Rugby Championship-winning team eight times.

- He has completed three Grand Slams against the Home Nations (Ireland, England, Scotland and Wales), in 2005, 2008 and 2010.

- He was a member of the Rugby World Cup-winning New Zealand team in 2011.

- In 2015 Carter signed a three-year deal to play for French Top 14 side Racing Metro.

Honours

Canterbury

National Provincial Championship/Air New Zealand Cup (4): 2004, 2008, 2009, 2010

Crusaders

Super Rugby champions (3): 2005, 2006, 2008
New Zealand Conference (1): 2011

Perpignan

Top 14 Championship (1): 2009

New Zealand

Tri Nations/Rugby Championship (8): 2003, 2005, 2006, 2007, 2008, 2010, 2012, 2013
British and Irish Lions tour (series victory) (1): 2005
Grand Slam Tour (3): 2005, 2008, 2010
Rugby World Cup (1): 2011
IRB Player of the Year (2): 2005, 2012

RICHIE McCAW (NEW ZEALAND)

- Richard 'Richie' Hugh McCaw was born on 31 December 1980.

- Known predominantly as an open-side flanker, he has also played as a blindside flanker and No. 8.

- He grew up in North Otago, before moving to Dunedin in 1994 to board at Otago Boys' High School. In 1999 he began his studies at Christ-church's Lincoln University and was selected in the national under-19 team.

- He made his debut for the Crusaders in Super Rugby in 2001.

- He was then selected for the All Blacks' 2001 tour, despite the fact that he had only played eight minutes of Super 12 rugby.

- His first appearance for New Zealand was a star-ring role against Ireland, and he was selected as New Zealand's first-choice open-side flanker for the 2003 World Cup.

- In 2006 he was appointed permanent captain of the All Blacks, whom he led at the 2007 World Cup. New Zealand were eliminated in the quarter-finals.

- He skippered the side to victory in the 2011 Rugby World Cup Final against France, in Eden Park, Auckland.

- McCaw had a very successful career with provincial side Canterbury, winning the NPC (later ITM Cup) six times. He also won the Super Rugby tournament on four occasions.

- In 2010 McCaw played his hundredth Super Rugby game and made a record-equalling ninety-fourth Test appearance for his country.

- In the 2011 World Cup pool game against France, McCaw reached a very special milestone. He became the first All Black to reach 100 caps.

- McCaw also became New Zealand's most capped All Black captain, having led the national team in eighty-seven Test matches. That eighty-seventh appearance as captain also led to him being the most capped Test captain in rugby union history.

- McCaw skippered New Zealand for the hundredth time against Wales in Cardiff, on 22 November 2014.

- He has been named the International Rugby Board International Player of the Year a record three times.

- New Zealand has lost only twelve Test matches with McCaw in the side.

- When the All Blacks faced the Springboks in Soweto in 2012, McCaw became the first rugby union player to win 100 Tests.

- His autobiography entitled *Richie McCaw: The*

Open Side was co-written by writer and playwright Greg McGee. In the United Kingdom and United States the book has a different title: *The Real McCaw.*

Honours

Canterbury

NPC/Air New Zealand Cup (6): 2001, 2004, 2008, 2009, 2010, 2011

Crusaders

Super Rugby champions (4): 2002, 2005, 2006, 2008

New Zealand

Tri Nations/Rugby Championship (9): 2002, 2003, 2005, 2006, 2007, 2008, 2010, 2012, 2013

British and Irish Lions tour (series victory) (1): 2005

Grand Slam Tour (3): 2005, 2008, 2010

Rugby World Cup (1): 2011

IRB Player of the Year (3): 2006, 2009, 2010

GARETH EDWARDS (WALES)

- Gareth Owen Edwards was born on 12 July 1947.

- Edwards was a miner's son from Gwaun-Cae-Gurwen, Wales.

- In addition to being a great rugby player, Edwards was a very talented athlete. He represented

West Wales Youth soccer team and then signed to Swansea Town at the age of sixteen. He also excelled at gymnastics and athletics.

- He made his debut for Cardiff RFC against Coventry on 17 September 1966. His career with Cardiff spanned twelve seasons, in which he scored sixty-nine tries in 195 games.

- Edwards won his first international cap for Wales on 1 April 1967. At the age of nineteen he took to the field against France in Paris. Wales lost 20–14 to the side that would go on to win the championship.

- Between 1967 and 1978 Edwards won caps in fifty-three successive matches for Wales, including thirteen as captain. He scored a total of twenty tries.

- Edwards was Wales' youngest ever captain. He skippered the side at the age of twenty, in February 1968, against Scotland. Wales won the match 5–0.

- He formed a fearsome partnership with two other Welsh legends, outside halves Barry John and Phil Bennett.

- Edwards' Welsh side dominated the Five Nations Championship, winning the crown seven times and amassing three Grand Slams.

- Edwards was voted player of the year in 1969, and in 1974 he was named BBC Wales Sports Personality of the Year.

- Edwards' career came full circle when he played his last match in 1978, when France again provided the opposition. This time he finished on the winning side, with a scoreline of 16–7 at the Arms Park in Cardiff. To put the icing on the cake, Wales also sealed the Grand Slam and a third consecutive Triple Crown.

- To top off a great year he was also named Rothmans Player of the Year 1978.

- He is one of a small group of Welsh players to have won three Grand Slams. They include Ryan Jones, Adam Jones, Gethin Jenkins, Gerald Davies and J. P. R. Williams.

- Edwards lined out ten times for the British and Irish Lions, playing for the legendary 1971 team, the only team to win a series in New Zealand. He was also a member of the unbeaten 1974 side in South Africa.

- In a poll conducted in 2003 by *Rugby World* magazine, Edwards was declared the greatest player of all time.

- Edwards' try for the Barbarians against the All Blacks in 1973 at Cardiff Arms Park is generally accepted as being one of the greatest of all time.

- When he penned his autobiography, he was termed a professional by the Welsh Rugby Football Union, as he would be paid for this, and was unable to coach or be involved in any way with the sport of rugby union.

– He was awarded an MBE in 1975, a CBE for his contribution to sport in 2007 and in June 2015 was given a knighthood for services to sport and charitable services in the Queen's Birthday Honours list.

– Edwards is also fondly remembered for his role as team captain on the TV quiz show *A Question of Sport*, along with much-loved Liverpool and England footballer Emlyn Hughes.

– In 1997 Edwards was one of the first fifteen former players inducted into the International Rugby Hall of Fame. He was joined by former partners in crime, Barry John and J. P. R. Williams.

– A plaque was erected to him in the Rugby Pathway of Fame in the town of Rugby, Warwickshire, where rugby is said to have first been played.

– Edwards was given the ultimate honour by his fellow countrymen when on 21 November 2001 he was voted the Greatest Welsh Player of All Time. The ceremony was held at the Cardiff International Arena by the Welsh Rugby Former International Players' Association.

– A sculpture of Gareth Edwards stands proudly in the St David's Centre, Cardiff.

Honours

Wales

Five Nations Championship (7): 1969, 1970, 1971, 1973, 1975, 1976, 1978

Grand Slam (3): 1971, 1976, 1978

Triple Crown (5): 1969, 1971, 1976, 1977, 1978

DAVID CAMPESE (AUSTRALIA)

–   David Ian Campese, nicknamed Campo, was born on the 21 October 1962 in Queanbeyan, New South Wales.

–   Campese was capped by the Wallabies 101 times in a career that began in 1982 and ended in 1996.

–   He held the world record for the most tries in Test matches (64) until overtaken by Japan's Daisuke Ohata, who scored his sixty-fifth try playing for Japan in 2006.

–   While Campese had a brilliant career, it was not without controversy. In the 1989 series against the British and Irish Lions, Australia were hot favourites to win, but a costly error by Campese gifted a try to the Lions. With the series tied at 1–1, he recklessly tried to run the ball from his own try line, then made a poor pass. The resulting turnover led to the Lions winning the Test, as well as the series. The part of the pitch where Campese lost the ball was dubbed 'Campo's Corner'.

- His nickname was 'Too Easy (Campese)'. The phrase 'Easy Campese' has become common in Australia, reflecting the free-spirited nature of his rugby playing style.

- He was voted the best player in the 1991 Rugby World Cup. He scored nine tries in Tests that season and six in the Rugby World Cup: two against Argentina, one against Wales and two against Ireland in the quarter-final, as the Wallabies stole the game at the death. He also scored in the semi-final victory against the defending champions, New Zealand.

- Campese spawned a new rugby term, the 'goose-step', a kicking motion in mid-run that changed his speed and disrupted the timing of opposing defenders attempting to tackle him.

- His final match was against the Barbarians, at Twickenham in 1996. He signed off with a typical defence-splitting run and try.

- Campese was part of the Australian team that conquered the All Blacks in New Zealand in 1986. The win ended a barren spell for the Aussies in New Zealand, which had lasted thirty-seven years.

- Campese won one of Australia's highest sporting awards in 1997, when he was inducted into the Sport Australia Hall of Fame.

- He was also the recipient of an Australian Sports Medal in 2000, a Centenary Medal in 2001, and was awarded Membership of the Order of Australia in 2002.

– In 2007 Campese was further honoured as he was one of the third set of inductees into the Australian Rugby Union Hall of Fame.

– Campese was also honoured on the world stage when he was inducted into the IRB (World Rugby) Hall of Fame in 2013.

– His autobiography was aptly entitled *On a Wing and a Prayer*.

Honours

Australia

Rugby World Cup (1): 1991

Bledisloe Cup (1): 1986

Rugby World Cup Player of the Tournament (1): 1991

JONAH LOMU (NEW ZEALAND)

– Jonah Tali Lomu, who is of Tongan descent, was born in Auckland on 12 May 1975.

– Lomu first came to notice in the prestigious Hong Kong Sevens tournament in 1994.

– He made a record-breaking start to his international career when he debuted on the wing against France in 1994. The match was played at

Lancaster Park in Christchurch, and the All Blacks lost 22–8.

- He was the All Blacks youngest ever player, at the age of nineteen years and forty-five days, breaking a record that had been held by Edgar Wrigley since 1905. He went on to win sixty-three caps.

- Lomu is the Rugby World Cup all-time top try scorer, with fifteen tries. Despite this, his team never won the trophy while he was playing.

- He has played for a number of domestic teams in Super Rugby and, later, the Magners League competitions. These include the Auckland Blues, Chiefs and Hurricanes, Counties Manukau, Wellington and, later, North Harbour, and Cardiff Blues.

- He played his first-ever World Cup match against Ireland in Johannesburg, scoring two tries in the 43–19 win.

- In the following match against Wales, Lomu struggled. He was replaced during the game and did not score any tries in the 34–9 victory.

- He did not feature in the final pool match against Japan. In the All Blacks' quarter-final, Lomu was back on the score sheet when he scored a try in the 48–30 win over Scotland at Loftus Versfeld.

- He duly made his mark on the World Cup in the

semi-final against England. In front of a stunned 51,000 packed into Newlands in Cape Town, he notched up four tries in the 45–29 defeat of the English. This included a try when he ran straight over the top of England full-back Mike Catt.

– Lomu struck gold for the Kiwis at the 1998 Commonwealth Games in Kuala Lumpur, in the rugby sevens event.

– Lomu is a member of the Champions for Peace club, a group of fifty-four famous elite athletes committed to promoting peace in the world through sport, created by Peace and Sport, a Monaco-based international organisation.

– Lomu kept his health problems a secret for many years. He struggled with nephrotic syndrome, a serious kidney disorder. The disease often left him confined to his bed between matches.

– He made a comeback from what seemed a career-ending kidney transplant in 2004. He underwent the transplant on 28 July 2004, in Auckland, New Zealand. The kidney was donated by Wellington radio presenter Grant Kereama.

– He was inducted into the International Rugby Hall of Fame on 9 October 2007 and was also inducted into the IRB Hall of Fame, on 24 October 2011.

– Lomu was awarded the New Zealand Order of Merit in the Queen's Birthday Honours list on 4 June 2007.

- Lomu is considered rugby's first-ever global superstar. His success spawned the video game *Jonah Lomu Rugby*.

Honours

New Zealand

Tri Nations/Rugby Championship (2): 1996, 1999

Commonwealth Games gold medal (1): 1998 (rugby sevens)

Bledisloe Cup (2): 1995, 1996

JONNY WILKINSON (ENGLAND)

- Jonathan Peter Wilkinson OBE was born on 25 May 1979.

- Wilkinson began his international career as an unused replacement against Scotland. He was then introduced as a sub for Mike Catt against Ireland, at Twickenham on 4 April 1998. He was eighteen at the time.

- Wilkinson made his full England debut against Australia in June 1998. England were hammered 76–0, which remains their biggest ever international defeat.

- He was a member of England's 2000 Six Nations-winning side and of the side that triumphed again in 2001.

- He set the individual Six Nations Championship point-scoring record, with 35 points against Italy at Twickenham in the 2001 championship, surpassing the best score achieved by his Newcastle Falcons mentor Rob Andrew.

- His best-remembered career highlight is his winning drop goal in the last minute of extra time against Australia in the 2003 Rugby World Cup final.

- Wilkinson was a member of the Lions touring side in 2001 (Australia) and 2005 (New Zealand). He scored 67 Test points in his six Lions Test games.

- England won sixty-seven of the ninety-one games that Wilkinson featured in.

- Wilkinson was renowned for his ability to drop goals. He scored a record twenty-ninth Test drop goal against France in the 2008 Six Nations.

- His first converted penalty against Scotland on 8 March 2008 made him the highest points scorer in international rugby. The kick took him three points past Wales' Neil Jenkins' tally of 1,090 Test rugby points. Wilkinson's points tally had been increased by 20 following the IRB decision to retrospectively grant full Test status to the 2005 British and Irish Lions warm-up Test against Argentina. Wilkinson had scored 20 points in that match, without which he would not have surpassed Jenkins' total on that day.

- On 26 February 2011 Wilkinson returned to the top of the international points-scoring charts. He overtook the then leader, Dan Carter of New Zealand, by scoring a penalty against France in a Six Nations match at Twickenham.

- He then passed Ronan O'Gara (522) to regain an overall points record total of 526 in the 2010 Six Nations Championship. When he retired from international rugby in 2011 his final Six Nations tally was 546, which has only been topped by O'Gara.

- Wilkinson holds the individual Rugby World Cup points record, with 277.

- In May 2013 he played an instrumental part in Toulon's 2013 Heineken Cup final victory. He scored 11 points in a 16–15 victory over fellow French Top 14 side Clermont Auvergne.

- Wilkinson was awarded ERC European Player of the Year for the 2013 tournament. He slotted over every place kick he took in the knockout stages (17) totalling an impressive 56 points for the knockouts alone. He amassed 108 points in total during the tournament.

- On 24 May 2014 he led Toulon to Heineken Cup glory as they defeated Saracens 23–6 in the 2014 final, scoring 13 of Toulon's points.

- On 31 May 2014, he led Toulon to the Top 14 final against Castres. Toulon won 18–10. Wilkinson kicked 15 points in what was to be the final game in a glittering career.

– Wilkinson was voted the BBC Sports Personality of the Year and IRB International Player of the Year in 2003.

– He is the only player to score points in two Rugby World Cup finals.

Honours

Newcastle Falcons
Premiership (1): 1998
Powergen Cup (2): 2001, 2004

Toulon
Heineken Cup (2): 2013, 2014
Top 14 (1): 2014

England
Rugby World Cup (1): 2003
Six Nations Championship (4): 2000, 2001, 2003, 2011
Grand Slam (1): 2003
Triple Crown (2): 2002, 2003

AROUND THE LEAGUES

GUINNESS PRO12 (formerly Rabo Direct Pro12)

–   In 2001, after an agreement between the Irish Rugby Football Union, Scottish Rugby Union and Welsh Rugby Union, a new competition called the Celtic League was formed, which would include the four Irish provinces.

–   Leinster and Munster contested the first final in 2002. Leinster took the spoils, edging their great rivals 24–20.

–   Irish giants Leinster, with four wins, Munster, with three, and Ulster with one make Ireland the most successful nation. The Ospreys have won four and Llanelli one, making five in total for Wales.

–   The first season saw a total of fifteen teams compete. They included the four Irish provinces (Connacht, Leinster, Munster and Ulster), two Scottish teams (Edinburgh Reivers and Glasgow) and all nine Welsh Premier Division teams (Bridgend, Caerphilly, Cardiff, Ebbw Vale, Llanelli, Neath, Newport, Pontypridd and Swansea).

–   The evolution of the Celtic League, had an impact on other competitions. The Scottish-Welsh League was abandoned in 2002. The Irish

Interprovincial Championship was also seen as no longer sustainable.

– The Celtic League began to grow in popularity in the early part of 2003, with the league becoming a commercial success. Welsh regional teams were struggling and now had only five fully professional clubs. A decision was taken that the Celtic League would become the sole professional league of the three countries, including all four Irish provinces.

– In 2003–04 the Celtic League became a twelve team league, which dropped to eleven the following year and then ten in the 2006–07 season. From the 2003–04 season on, the winners were decided by league points rather than a final.

– In May 2006 Magners Irish Cider was named as the competition sponsor for the next five seasons, and the league was renamed the Magners League.

– Leinster v Ulster on 31 December 2006 was the final rugby match played at Lansdowne Road before it was redeveloped as the Aviva Stadium.

– The 2009–10 season was the last ten-team league (with the entry of Italian teams the following year), and the format was also changed, with semi-finals and a grand final replacing the league table final standings.

- In the 2012 grand final at the RDS in Dublin, the Ospreys caused a sensation by defeating red-hot favourites Leinster and winning the title. It was their first win in Dublin in five years.

- The league was sponsored by Rabo Direct bank from 2012 to 2014. The Pro12 name was adopted to reflect the new multinational league.

- Tommy Bowe of Ulster and formerly Ospreys has scored fifty-six tries, a competition record.

- Tim Visser of Edinburgh scored a record fourteen tries in one season.

- Felipe Contepomi holds the season points record, with 276 points.

Roll of Honour

Season	Winners	Runners-up
2002	Leinster	Munster
2003	Munster	Neath
2004	Llanelli	Ulster
2005	Ospreys	Cardiff Blues
2006	Ulster	Leinster
2007	Ospreys	Cardiff Blues
2008	Leinster	Cardiff Blues
2009	Munster	Edinburgh
2010	Ospreys	Leinster
2011	Munster	Leinster
2012	Ospreys	Leinster

2013	Leinster	Ulster
2014	Leinster	Glasgow Warriors
2015	Glasgow Warriors	Munster

ENGLISH AVIVA PREMIERSHIP

- There are twelve clubs in the Premiership. The competition has been played since 1987.

- The clubs involved in the first season, 1987–88, were Bath, Bristol, Coventry, Gloucester, Harlequins, Leicester, Moseley, Nottingham, Orrell, Sale, Wasps and Waterloo. They arranged their matches on mutually convenient dates.

- The top flight league has evolved since it was introduced in 1987–88. From 1987–97, this was known as the Courage League, comprising twelve clubs at the top of a league pyramid with roughly 1,000 clubs playing in 108 leagues, each with promotion and relegation.

- Since the start of the first league in 1987–88, Leicester have been the kingpins of Premiership rugby, with ten wins. Bath and London Wasps are in second spot on six wins each.

- The league turned professional for the 1996–97 season. The first champions were London Wasps.

- What is now the Aviva Premiership (since 2010) runs from September to May and is made up of twenty-two rounds of matches. Each club plays each of its rivals, in both home and away matches.

– From the first season to the 1999–2000 season, the winner of the league competition also won the premiership. However, from 2000–01, a semi-final and final stage was introduced, featuring the four teams at the top of the league table.

– Following the completion of the regular season, the top four teams go into a play-off. The top two teams from the league have the benefit of home advantage. The leaders host the fourth-ranked team. The winners of the semi-finals then advance to the final, which is always held at Twickenham Stadium. The winners become the Premiership champions.

– Gloucester have finished top of the league on three occasions (2003, 2007, 2008) and failed to go on to win the title.

– Harlequins won the title the first time they reached the final, in 2012. Only six other clubs have won the Premiership since its beginning in 1996–97. They are: Newcastle Falcons, London Wasps, Leicester Tigers, Sale Sharks, Northampton Saints and Saracens.

– Since 2004 Round 1 of the new season has included the London Double Header, usually featuring the four London teams, at Twickenham Stadium. In 2013 it had an attendance of over 60,000.

- A new format in the Premiership sees the top six teams in the table qualify directly for the following season's Champions Cup. The seventh-placed team advances to a play-off for another Champions Cup place. In the cup competition they face teams from the French Top 14 and the Guinness Pro12.

- Former England international Charlie Hodgson of Sale and Saracens holds the record for the most points scored, with 2,469.

- Steve Borthwick of Bath and Saracens has made the most appearances in the league, with 265.

- Mark Cueto of Sale holds the most tries record, with ninety.

- Mike Watson created an unwelcome piece of Premiership history when playing as a second-row forward for London Scottish. His sending off after 42 seconds, the fastest ever, handed Bath an easy win, 76–13.

- It was also London Scottish's last Premiership game before being placed into administration, and to date they have not returned to the top tier of English rugby.

- In 2013 Nick Wood of Gloucester became the second-fastest red-carded player. He was given his marching orders after 73 seconds in a game against Saracens, which Wood's side lost 44–12.

Premiership Finals

Season	Winners	Score	Runners-up	Attendance
2000–01	Leicester Tigers	22–10	Bath	33,500
2001–02	Gloucester	28–23	Bristol	28,500
2002–03	London Wasps	39–3	Gloucester	42,000
2003–04	London Wasps	10–6	Bath	59,500
2004–05	London Wasps	39–14	Leicester Tigers	66,000
2005–06	Sale Sharks	45–20	Leicester Tigers	58,000
2006–07	Leicester Tigers	44–16	Gloucester	59,000
2007–08	London Wasps	26–16	Leicester Tigers	81,600
2008–09	Leicester Tigers	10–9	London Irish	81,601
2009–10	Leicester Tigers	33–27	Saracens	81,600
2010–11	Saracens	22–18	Leicester Tigers	80,016
2011–12	Harlequins	30–23	Leicester Tigers	81,779
2012–13	Leicester Tigers	37–17	Northampton Saints	81,703
2013–14	Northampton Saints	24–20 (a.e.t.)	Saracens	81,193
2014–15	Saracens	28–16	Bath	80,589

THE FRENCH TOP 14

–   The competition was previously known as the Top 16.

–   There is promotion and relegation in the division as two teams from the next division, the Rugby Pro D2, are promoted and the two bottom teams of the Top 14 are relegated.

–   The first-ever final, a one-off championship game, took place in 1892, before a crowd of 2,000 people, with a very famous referee. The match official was Baron Pierre de Coubertin, the founder of the International Olympic Committee. The game was between two Paris-based sides, Stade Français and Racing Club, with the latter becoming the first-ever champions. The final score read more like a soccer match – 4–3!

–   The competition has been held on an annual basis since then, excepting the years 1915–19 and 1940–42 when it was not played due to the two World Wars.

–   Toulouse has been the competition's most successful club, winning nineteen times.

–   Lourdes won the delayed 1968 championship in unusual circumstances. Having drawn 6–6 and 9–9 (a.e.t.) with Toulon, they were awarded the title. They had scored two tries while Toulon had scored none, and there was no remaining time to reschedule a third final, because the French national team was due to go on tour to New Zealand and South Africa shortly afterwards.

- Toulouse has won a total of 217 matches since the birth of the professional competition in 1996, the most of any side. Perpignan is in second place with 188 wins.

- The domestic season runs from August through to June. Every club contests twenty-six games during the regular season.

Roll of Honour

Stade Toulousain (19): 1912, 1922, 1923, 1924, 1926, 1927, 1947, 1985, 1986, 1989, 1994, 1995, 1996, 1997, 1999, 2001, 2008, 2011, 2012

Stade Français (14): 1893, 1894, 1895, 1897, 1898, 1901, 1903, 1905, 1998, 2000, 2003, 2004, 2007, 2015

AS Béziers (11): 1961, 1971, 1972, 1974, 1975, 1977, 1978, 1980, 1981, 1983, 1984

Union Bordeaux Bègles* (9): 1899 (as SBUC), 1904 (as SBUC), 1905 (as SBUC), 1906 (as SBUC), 1907 (as SBUC), 1909 (as SBUC), 1911 (as SBUC), 1969 (as CAB), 1991 (as CAB)

SU Agen (8): 1930, 1945, 1962, 1965, 1966, 1976, 1982, 1988

FC Lourdes (8): 1948, 1952, 1953, 1956, 1957, 1958, 1960, 1968

USA Perpignan (7): 1914, 1921, 1925, 1938, 1944, 1955, 2009

Racing Club de France (5): 1892, 1900, 1902, 1959, 1990

Biarritz Olympique (5): 1935, 1939, 2002, 2005, 2006

Castres Olympique (4): 1949, 1950, 1993, 2013

RC Toulonnais (4): 1931, 1987, 1992, 2014

Aviron Bayonnais (3): 1913, 1934, 1943

Section Paloise (3): 1928, 1946, 1964

Stadoceste Tarbais (2): 1920, 1973

Narbonne (2): 1936, 1979

Lyon (2): 1932, 1933

ASM Clermont Auvergne (1): 2010

Stade Montois (1): 1963

US Quillan (1): 1929

Olympique de Pantin (1): 1896

FC Grenoble (1): 1954

CS Vienne (1): 1937

La Voulte sportif (1): 1970

US Montauban (1): 1967

US Carmaux (1): 1951

FC Lyon (1): 1910

* Bordeaux Bègles merged with Stade Bordelais UC (SBUC) in 2005. Union Bordeaux Bègles was the new name for the merged team. Bordeaux used to be known as Club Athlétique Bordeaux-Bègles Gironde, CAB for short. The shortened names show which entity of each team won what and when!

SUPER RUGBY

- Super Rugby, formerly known as the Super 12 and the Super 14, is the premier club rugby competition in the southern hemisphere.

- The original competition dates back to 1986, when the South Pacific Championship was formed with teams from a number of southern-hemisphere nations.

- The inaugural competition featured just six teams: Auckland, Canterbury and Wellington (New Zealand); Queensland and New South Wales (Australia); and a composite Fijian side. In 1993 the format changed with the addition of South African sides and it became the Super 10.

- The competition known as the Super 12 ran from 1996 to 2005. It then changed to the Super 14, with the addition of a further two teams for the 2006 season. The competition was further expanded to fifteen teams for the 2011 season, five from New Zealand, Australia and South Africa apiece. It was then rebranded as Super Rugby.

- SANZAR, who also run the Rugby Championship, operate the competition.

- The first Super 14 final was played at Lancaster Park, in Christchurch, on 27 May 2006. In an all-New Zealand clash, Crusaders defeated the Hurricanes 19–12.

- The trophy has three curved legs for each Conference involved in the competition. Coloured strips on the legs represent the competing nations – gold for Australia, black for New Zealand and green for the South Africa.

- Doug Howlett is the top try scorer in the competition, with fifty-nine.

- Daniel Carter holds the record for the most points scored (1,705), for the Crusaders.

- Kevin Mealamu of the Auckland Blues has made the most appearances (163).

- Caleb Ralph made 103 consecutive appearances for the Crusaders.

- South African out-half Morné Steyn of the Bulls holds a number of season-long records. They include: most points (263) and most penalties (51), both from 2010. He also set the drop-goal record (11) in 2009.

Super Rugby Teams (geographic sources)

Australia

New South Waratahs: Northern and Central New South Wales, including Sydney, Newcastle, Wollongong, Tamworth and Coffs Harbour.

Brumbies: Australian Capital Territory and Southern New South Wales, including Canberra, Queanbeyan, Nowra and Albury.

Western Force: all of Western Australia, including Perth, Mandurah, Bunbury and Kalgoorlie.

Queensland Reds: all of Queensland, including Brisbane, Gold Coast, Cairns and Rockhampton.

Melbourne Rebels: all of Victoria, including Greater Melbourne, Geelong and the Surf Coast, the Western Districts and the Mallee, Sunraysia south of the Murray, the Central Goldfields of Ballarat and Bendigo, and Gippsland.

New Zealand

Auckland Blues: Auckland, North Harbour and Northland, North Auckland Peninsula of North Island and most of metropolitan Auckland.

Highlanders: North Otago, Otago and Southland, Southern South Island, including Dunedin and Invercargill.

Hurricanes: East Coast, Hawke's Bay, Horowhenua Kapiti, Manawatu, Poverty Bay, Wairarapa-Bush, Wanganui and Wellington, southern and south-western North Island, including Wellington, Palmerston North and Napier.

Chiefs: Bay of Plenty, Counties Manukau, Taranaki, King Country, Thames Valley and Waikato, central and eastern North Island (including Hamilton), southern Auckland, Tauranga, Rotorua and New Plymouth.

Crusaders: Buller, Canterbury, Mid Canterbury, South Canterbury, Tasman and West Coast, north and central South Island, including Christchurch, Nelson, Blenheim and Timaru.

South Africa

Bulls: Pretoria, East Rand and Limpopo Province.

Stormers: Cape Town and northern Western Cape.

Sharks: Durban and KwaZulu-Natal.

Central Cheetahs: Bloemfontein, Free State and Northern Cape.

Lions: Johannesburg, Mpumalanga and North West.

WINNERS TABLE

Year	Winners	Score	Runners-up
1996	Blues	45–21	Sharks
1997	Blues	23–7	Brumbies
1998	Crusaders	20–13	Blues
1999	Crusaders	24–19	Highlanders
2000	Crusaders	20–19	Brumbies
2001	Brumbies	36–6	Sharks
2002	Crusaders	31–13	Brumbies
2003	Blues	21–17	Crusaders
2004	Brumbies	47–38	Crusaders
2005	Crusaders	35–25	Waratahs
2006	Crusaders	19–12	Hurricanes
2007	Bulls	20–19	Sharks
2008	Crusaders	20–12	Waratahs
2009	Bulls	61–17	Chiefs
2010	Bulls	25–17	Stormers
2011	Reds	18–13	Crusaders
2012	Chiefs	37–6	Sharks
2013	Chiefs	27–22	Brumbies
2014	Waratahs	33–32	Crusaders

IRISH WOMEN'S RUGBY

- Women's international rugby union has a history going back to the late nineteenth century, but it was not until 13 June 1982 that the first international fixture (or Test match) took place. The match was organised in connection with the Dutch Rugby Union's fiftieth anniversary.

- The Irish women's international team play their home games at Ashbourne, County Meath. They played their first international against Scotland in Edinburgh on Valentine's Day 1993. The Scots emerged victorious on a 10–0 scoreline.

- Unlike men's rugby, there is no official ranking of women's teams. Generally the IRB refers to the placings in the preceding World Cup. However, Rugby Europe (originally the Fédération Internationale de Rugby Amateur) compiles an annual ranking of European teams and rugby.

- The largest margin of victory for the Irish women was in 2004. They scored 55 unanswered points against Japan.

- Their heaviest defeat came at the hands of England, in Worcester on 17 February 2002 (79–0).

- Ireland have contested five World Cups. Until 2014 their best performance came when they finished seventh. In the 2014 competition they bettered that by reaching the play-off for third place. They lost out to France, but still achieved a highest-ever fourth-place finish.

– Ireland won their first Six Nations Grand Slam in 2013 and in 2015 they won the championship.

– New Zealand-born Tania Rosser won her fiftieth Irish cap against her native New Zealand in the 2014 Rugby World Cup, in Paris. Ireland caused a major shock when they defeated the Black Ferns 17–14 in their Pool B encounter. It was the first time an Irish international senior team had defeated a New Zealand side. Tries by Heather O'Brien and Alison Miller and a brilliant place-kicking performance from Niamh Briggs stunned the Kiwis, who had won the previous four World Cup tournaments.

RESULTS SUMMARY (full internationals only)

Opponent	Played	Won	Lost	Drew
Australia	2	0	2	0
Canada	2	1	1	0
England	20	2	18	0
France	22	2	19	1
Germany	3	3	0	0
Italy	13	12	1	0
Japan	3	2	1	0
Kazakhstan	4	1	3	0
Netherlands	3	3	0	0

New Zealand	1	1	0	0
Samoa	1	0	1	0
Scotland	24	10	14	0
South Africa	1	1	0	0
Spain	9	4	5	0
USA	7	3	4	0
Wales	21	9	12	0
Total	**136**	**54**	**81**	**1**

WOMEN'S RUGBY WORLD CUP RESULTS

1991

Winners: United States (19–6)

Runners-up: England

Third: France

Fourth: New Zealand

1994

Winners: England (38–23)

Runners-up: USA

Third: France

Fourth: Wales

1998

Winners: New Zealand (44–12)

Runners-up: USA

Third: England

Fourth: Canada

2002

Winners: New Zealand (19–9)

Runners-up: England

Third: France

Fourth: Canada

2006

Winners: New Zealand (25–17)

Runners-up: England

Third: France

Fourth: Canada

2010

Winners: New Zealand (13–10)

Runners-up: England

Third: Australia

Fourth: France

2014

Winners: England (21–9)

Runners-up: Canada

Third: France

Fourth: Ireland

FAMOUS RUGBY GROUNDS

THOMOND PARK

- Thomond Park stadium is located in Limerick city, with Munster Rugby, Shannon RFC and UL Bohemian RFC as tenants.

- The capacity of the stadium is 25,600, following the redevelopment completed in 2008.

- The stadium has hosted just six international fixtures in well over a century. The first was Ireland v Wales on 19 March 1898. The most recent was Ireland v Fiji, in the Guinness Autumn Series of 2012.

- The stadium is famed for its raucous sporting crowd, who provide impressive noise during play and complete silence when home or away players are kicking for goal.

- Munster Rugby turned the stadium into a fortress during a twelve-year unbeaten run at Thomond in the Heineken Cup. This period ran from the competition's start in 1995 until 2007. Leicester Tigers broke the streak with a 13–6 win.

- Thomond Park was the scene of one of the sport's greatest-ever upsets – Munster upstaging the legendary All Blacks in 1978. New Zealand were remarkably held scoreless, as a Tony Ward-led home side won 12–0.

- Munster's average league attendance for the 2013–14 Pro12 season was 12,195.

- The iconic stadium was due to be renamed in a sponsorship deal following its redevelopment. However, it was confirmed in February 2008 that the Thomond Park name would be retained, with the naming rights to the individual stands being sold instead.

- When rugby blog intheloose provided a list of its top five rugby stadiums in the world, they were forced to add Thomond to the list after the wave of response they got demanding its inclusion.

- The Republic of Ireland football team played two international friendlies in Thomond Park during the construction of the Aviva Stadium. The first, on 12 August 2009, was against Australia, which the visitors won 3–0. On 8 September 2009 Ireland defeated South Africa 1–0.

- The Irish heats for the 2011 Special Olympics World Summer Games took place in Thomond over four days in June 2010.

- The stadium hosted its first rugby league game on 5 November 2011. Ireland took on France but lost 16–34.

- On 9 November 2013 Ireland played their Rugby League World Cup Group A match against Australia in Thomond Park, but were convincingly beaten 50–0.

- Thomond is also a popular concert venue, with the likes of Elton John, Rod Stewart, Bob Dylan and Bruce Springsteen performing there in recent years.

EDEN PARK

- Eden Park, Auckland, was originally a cricket ground and was first called the Kingsland Cricket Ground and then Eden Cricket Ground.

- Auckland Rugby took out a twenty-one-year lease on the ground in 1914.

- The first rugby Test match was held on 27 August 1921. The game was between South Africa and New Zealand. The Springboks won by a 9–5 margin in front of an attendance of 40,000 spectators.

- Eden Park is the largest sports stadium in New Zealand. The ground has a permanent capacity of 50,000. This rose to 60,000 during the 2011 Rugby World Cup, as temporary seating was added.

- In 1981 the third Test match between New Zealand and South Africa was played at Eden Park. Before the game took place, the ground was flour-bombed by anti-apartheid protesters.

- Eden Park is the home ground of the Auckland Blues Super Rugby franchise.

- The ground played host to a Rugby League World Cup Final in 1988, one year after it hosted the final of the 1987 Rugby Union World Cup.

- A $256-million redevelopment of Eden Park was completed in 2010. The ground is now all seated, with no standing areas.

LANSDOWNE ROAD (now Aviva Stadium)

- Lansdowne Road Stadium was the brainchild of Henry Wallace Doveton Dunlop. Dunlop, who was the organiser of the first All-Ireland Athletics Championships, was a graduate of engineering from Trinity College Dublin. He also founded Lansdowne Football Club in 1872, and the ground was home to the famous Irish club side.

- Wanderers Football Club, which was founded in 1870, joined Lansdowne at the grounds later.

- The first rugby match held at Lansdowne was an interprovincial fixture between Leinster and Ulster in December 1876.

- On 11 March 1878 Lansdowne Road hosted one of the first international rugby fixtures, against England, making it the world's oldest rugby union Test venue until its demolition in 2007.

- The first victory Ireland had at the ground took place on 5 February 1887 against England.

- The first international soccer match at the venue,

on St Patrick's Day 1900, saw England beat Ireland 2–0.

- The IRFU erected its first covered stand in 1908 on the railway side of the pitch.

- After the First World War a memorial to the IRFU members who died in the fighting was erected on one of the stadium's walls. It is now located outside the media centre at the Aviva Stadium.

- In 1952 the first-ever rugby Colours Match between University College Dublin and Trinity College Dublin took place there.

- In 1954 the Upper West Stand was erected at Lansdowne, creating 8,000 additional seats. This led to the stadium becoming the permanent home of Irish rugby.

- The stadium regularly hosted athletics meetings and in the 1950s Olympic gold medallist Ronnie Delany raced there against the great athletes of that era, including Brian Hewson and Derek Ibbotsen.

- The meeting of Waterford FC and Manchester United in the 1968–69 European Cup, in September 1968, was the first-ever football club match to be played at the venue.

- In 1977 the West Lower Stand was demolished and replaced. The uncovered stand at the corner of the North Terrace was demolished and the terracing was extended.

- On 20 November 1988 Boston College beat Army 38–24 in what was dubbed the Emerald Isle Classic. It was the first major American football game ever played in Europe, played before 42,525 fans at the stadium. It was estimated at the time that the game brought nearly US$30 million in spending to the local economy.

- The last international rugby match before the demolition of Lansdowne Road was a 61–17 Ireland win over the Pacific Islanders, on 26 November 2006.

- The last ever rugby action at the old Lansdowne Road Stadium was a game that took place on 31 December 2006. Leinster beat Ulster 20–12 in a Magners League encounter. The game set a record attendance of 48,000 for a league match.

- The demolition of the stadium began in May 2007. The new Aviva Stadium opened on 14 May 2010 with a capacity of 51,700.

MURRAYFIELD (now the BT Murrayfield Stadium)

- Murrayfield is the fourth-largest stadium in the United Kingdom.

- In 1994 a £50-million renovation of Murrayfield was completed, during which floodlights were installed for the first time.

- The stadium is located in the West End of Edinburgh. It has an all-seated capacity of 67,144. The capacity was reduced recently from 67,800 to accommodate the largest permanent big screens in the country.

- Before Murrayfield was opened on 21 March 1925, Scottish internationals were staged at Inverleith. Murrayfield's first visitors were England, for that year's Five Nations Championship. Scotland were victorious, claiming their first Grand Slam.

- During the Second World War the ground at Murrayfield was used by the Royal Army Service Corps as a supply depot. During the war years the armed forces sports authorities arranged two Scotland v England services internationals every year, on a home-and-away basis. Scotland's home matches once again had to be played at Inverleith, until Murrayfield was derequisitioned in 1944.

- Murrayfield set a world-record match attendance of 104,000 on 1 March 1975, when Scotland defeated Wales 12–10 during the Five Nations Championship. This record would stand until August 1999, when 107,042 people attended a Bledisloe Cup game between Australia and New Zealand at the Olympic Stadium in Sydney. The Murrayfield attendance record still stands as the highest attendance for a European rugby game and the all-time third-highest world attendance.

RAVENHILL

– Ravenhill is the home of Ulster Rugby. With the opening of a new stand for the 2014 Heineken Cup quarter-final against Saracens on 5 April 2014, the capacity of the stadium is now 18,196.

– Ravenhill Stadium opened in 1923. It features an ornate arch at the entrance, which was erected as a war memorial to players killed in the two World Wars.

– Before 1923 Ulster played their home games at the Royal Ulster Agricultural Society grounds in the Balmoral area of Belfast.

– Ravenhill hosted pool games in both the 1991 and 1999 Rugby World Cups.

– Ravenhill has hosted eighteen international matches. The most recent Ireland international played at the stadium was on 24 August 2007. The game was against Italy in a warm-up for the 2007 Rugby World Cup.

– Ireland played Scotland in the last ever Five Nations Championship match to be played at Ravenhill, in 1954.

– Ravenhill has also played host to the Under 19 Rugby World Championship final. New Zealand defeated South Africa back in 2007.

– Ravenhill has been the scene of many glorious

Ulster triumphs, including a memorable defeat of French giants Toulouse 15–13 in the 1999 Heineken Cup.

–   Ravenhill also hosted the 1999 Heineken Cup semi-final. Ulster took another French scalp when they defeated Stade Français 33–27.

–   In 2014 Ulster signed a ten-year contract with the Kingspan Group. The stadium will be known as the Kingspan Stadium until 2024.

TWICKENHAM

–   Twickenham Stadium is located in Richmond upon Thames, London. It is the largest stadium in the world to be devoted solely to the sport of rugby union.

–   Twickenham is the fifth-largest stadium in Europe and the second-biggest in the UK.

–   The first game played there was on 2 October 1909, between Harlequins and Richmond, and the stadium celebrated its centenary during the 2009–10 season.

–   Wales were the visitors for a special hundredth anniversary of the first international game at Twickenham in 1910. England wore a special commemorative shirt for the fixture. Iain Spragg penned a book to mark the event, entitled *Twickenham: 100 Years of Rugby's HQ*.

- England Rugby Union Treasurer William Cail played a leading role in the purchase of the land at Twickenham in 1907, for £5,500 12s 6d. Before the purchase the land was used to grow cabbages. It is still known as 'the Cabbage Patch' today.

- During the First World War the ground was mainly used for cattle, horse and sheep grazing. King George V unveiled a special war memorial at the grounds in 1921.

- A special game was played in 1959 to mark fifty years of the ground. A combined side of England and Wales beat Ireland and Scotland 26–17.

- In the last match of the 1988 season, against the Irish, England were 0–3 down at half-time. In the second half they produced a remarkable turnaround to score six tries and win 35–3. It was on that day that 'Swing Low, Sweet Chariot' was adopted as a terrace song.

CARDIFF ARMS PARK

- The architect of the stadium was Archibald Leitch, who also designed Goodison Park, Ibrox Stadium and Old Trafford, among others.

- 1882 saw the construction of the first stands; they held 300 spectators and cost £50 to build.

- The Arms Park was host to the Commonwealth

Games in 1958. It also hosted four games in the 1991 Rugby World Cup, including the third-place play-off.

- The Arms Park was the venue for the first-ever Heineken Cup final, in 1996. The stadium also held the following season's decider.

- Both rugby and cricket were originally played at the grounds.

- Redevelopment of the stadium began in 1968 and the grounds were renamed the National Stadium. It was officially opened on 7 April 1984.

- On 7 May 1988, what was then a world-record crowd for a club game, 56,000, attended the clash between Llanelli and Neath in the final of the Schweppes Cup.

- The first game played under floodlights was held on 4 September 1991 between Wales and France.

- The last international match held at the National Stadium was the Five Nations match between Wales and England on 15 March 1997.

- The last ever match held at the National Stadium was on 26 April 1997 between Welsh rivals Cardiff and Swansea. Cardiff won the SWALEC Cup 33–26.

- The Millennium Stadium opened in June 1999. In a friendly international to mark the occasion, Wales defeated South Africa by 29–9.

HEINEKEN CUP HISTORY

- The Heineken Cup (known as the H Cup in France due to restrictions on alcohol sponsorship) was one of two annual European rugby union competitions run by European Club Rugby from 1995 to 2014.

- The first-ever Heineken Cup match took place in Romania. Toulouse defeated Farul Constanța 54–10 in front of a small crowd. From there the competition gathered momentum and crowds grew.

- The competition was sponsored by Dutch brewing company Heineken International from its launch in 1995.

- Twelve clubs from Ireland, France, Wales, Italy and Romania took part in the inaugural 1995–96 tournament. English and Scottish teams joined the following year bringing the number of teams to twenty, although Romania did not feature after the first year of the competition.

- The tournament was launched in the summer of 1995 on the initiative of the then Five Nations committee to provide a new level of professional cross-border competition.

- In the first Heineken Cup, the twelve sides competed in four pools of three, with the group winners going directly into the semi-finals. The following year there were four pools of five. In the 1999–2000 season it grew to twenty-four clubs.

- Toulouse became the first Heineken Cup winners, eventually beating Cardiff in extra time in front of a crowd of 21,800 at Cardiff Arms Park.

- The Heineken Cup was open to clubs from the Celtic League (now the RaboDirect Pro12), the Aviva Premiership and the Top 14.

- The Italian Eccellenza competition also sent clubs into the Heineken Cup in the 2009 and 2010 seasons but ceased to do so after the Celtic League expanded to include Italian franchises.

- Clubs in Europe's top leagues that did not qualify for the Heineken Cup entered the second-tier European Challenge Cup (also known as the Amlin Challenge Cup), along with teams from outside the top European rugby nations.

- Of the twenty-four places in the Heineken Cup, twenty-two were awarded by country (with each country deciding how to allocate their places), one was decided by a play-off between an Italian and Celtic League team and one was allocated to the French, Italian or English team that progressed the most in the previous year's competition.

- Toulouse have won the competition a record four times.

- The tournament was won by Leinster three times, while Munster, Leicester Tigers, Toulon and London Wasps all won it twice.

- The European Rugby Champions Cup replaced the Heineken Cup at the start of the 2014–15 season.

- Toulon became the first side to win Europe's premier rugby competition three times in a row, when they defeated Clermont Auvergne in 2015.

Heineken Cup/European Champions Cup Results

Season	Winners	Score	Runners-up	Venue	Attendance
1996	Toulouse	21–18	Cardiff	Cardiff Arms Park	21,800
1997	Brive	28–9	Leicester Tigers	Cardiff Arms Park	41,664
1998	Bath	19–18	Brive	Parc Lescure	36,500
1999	Ulster	21–6	Colomiers	Lansdowne Road	49,000
2000	Northampton Saints	9–8	Munster	Twickenham Stadium	68,441
2001	Leicester Tigers	34–30	Stade Français	Parc des Princes	44,000
2002	Leicester Tigers	15–9	Munster	Millennium Stadium	74,000
2003	Toulouse	22–17	Perpignan	Lansdowne Road	28,600
2004	London Wasps	27–20	Toulouse	Twickenham	73,057
2005	Toulouse	18–12	Stade Français	Murrayfield	51,326
2006	Munster	23–19	Biarritz	Millennium Stadium	74,534

Season	Winners	Score	Runners-up	Venue	Attendance
2007	London Wasps	25–9	Leicester Tigers	Twickenham	81,076
2008	Munster	16–13	Toulouse	Millennium Stadium	74,417
2009	Leinster	19–16	Leicester Tigers	Murrayfield	66,523
2010	Toulouse	21–19	Biarritz	Stade de France	78,962
2011	Leinster	33–22	Northampton Saints	Millennium Stadium	72,456
2012	Leinster	42–14	Ulster	Twickenham	81,774
2013	Toulon	16–15	Clermont Auvergne	Aviva Stadium	51,142
2014	Toulon	23–6	Saracens	Millennium Stadium	67,578
2015	Toulon	24–18	Clermont Auvergne	Twickenham	56, 622

Roll of Honour

Toulouse (4): 1996, 2003, 2005, 2010

Leinster (3): 2009, 2011, 2012

Toulon (3): 2013, 2014, 2015

Leicester Tigers (2): 2001, 2002

Munster (2): 2006, 2008

London Wasps (2): 2004, 2007

Brive (1): 1997

Northampton Saints (1): 2000

Ulster (1): 1999

Bath (1): 1998

Try-scoring Records

Vincent Clerc (Toulouse): 36

Brian O'Driscoll (Leinster): 33

Dafydd James (Pontypridd, Llanelli, Bridgend, Celtic Warriors, Harlequins, Scarlets): 29

Shane Horgan (Leinster): 27

Chris Ashton (Northampton Saints, Saracens): 27

Gordon D'Arcy (Leinster): 26

Tommy Bowe (Ulster, Ospreys): 26

Geordan Murphy (Leicester Tigers): 25

Napolioni Nalaga (ASM Clermont): 25

Ben Cohen (Northampton Saints, Brive, Sale Sharks): 24

Michel Marfaing (Toulouse): 24

Anthony Foley (Munster): 23

Tom Voyce (Bath, London Wasps, Gloucester): 23

Top Points Scorers

Ronan O'Gara (Munster): 1,365

Stephen Jones (Llanelli, Clermont Auvergne, Scarlets): 869

Dimitri Yachvili (Biarritz): 661

Diego Domínguez (Milan, Stade Français): 645

David Humphreys (Ulster): 564

Neil Jenkins (Pontypridd, Cardiff, Celtic Warriors): 502

David Skrela (Colomiers, Stade Français, Toulouse, Clermont Auvergne): 500

Andy Goode (Leicester Tigers, Saracens, Brive, Wasps): 483

Dan Parks (Glasgow Warriors, Cardiff Blues, Connacht): 479

Johnny Sexton (Leinster, Racing Metro): 458

Felipe Contepomi (Bristol, Leinster, Toulon): 444

Jean-Baptiste Elissalde (Toulouse): 441

Appearances

Ronan O'Gara (Munster): 110

Gordon D'Arcy (Leinster): 104

John Hayes (Munster): 101

Peter Stringer (Munster, Saracens, Bath): 100

Donncha O'Callaghan (Munster): 96

Leo Cullen (Leinster, Leicester Tigers): 92

Clément Poitrenaud (Toulouse): 91

Shane Horgan (Leinster): 87

Brian O'Driscoll (Leinster): 87

Nathan Hines (Sale Sharks): 87

Anthony Foley (Munster): 86

David Wallace (Munster): 86

CAPS, AWARDS AND HALL OF FAME

MOST CAPPED INTERNATIONAL PLAYERS

141 Brian O'Driscoll   1999–2014   Centre
Ireland (133), British and Irish Lions (8)

139 George Gregan   1994–2007   Scrum-half
Australia

138 Richie McCaw   2001–   Flanker
New Zealand

130 Ronan O'Gara   2000–13   Fly-half
Ireland (128), British and Irish Lions (2)

123 Keven Mealamu   2002–   Hooker
New Zealand

121 Victor Matfield   2001–   Lock
South Africa

119 Gethin Jenkins   2002–   Prop
Wales (114), British and Irish Lions (5)

119 Jason Leonard   1990–2004   Prop
England (114), British and Irish Lions (5)

118 Fabien Pelous   1995–2007   Lock
France

116 Nathan Sharpe   2002–12   Lock
Australia

112	Sergio Parisse Italy	2002–	Number 8
111	Marco Bortolami Italy	2001–	Lock
111	Philippe Sella France	1982–95	Centre
111	John Smit South Africa	2000–2011	Hooker
111	George Smith Australia	2000–13	Flanker
110	Stephen Jones Wales (104), British and Irish Lions (6)	1998–2011	Fly-half
110	Tony Woodcock New Zealand	2002–	Prop
110	Martin Castrogiovanni Italy	2002–	Prop
109	Chris Paterson Scotland	1999–2011	Utility back
108	Paul O'Connell Ireland (101), British and Irish Lions (7)	2002–	Lock
107	John Hayes Ireland (105), British and Irish Lions (2)	2000–11	Prop
106	Jean de Villiers South Africa	2004–	Centre

106	Bryan Habana	2002–	Wing
	South Africa		
104	Adam Ashley-Cooper	2005–	Centre
	Australia		
104	Martyn Williams	1996–2012	Flanker
	Wales (100), British and Irish Lions (4)		
103	Andrea Lo Cicero Vaina	2000–13	Prop
	Italy		
103	Gareth Thomas	1995–2007	Back
	Wales (100), British and Irish Lions (3)		
102	Stephen Larkham	1996–2007	Fly-half
	Australia		
102	Percy Montgomery	1997–2008	Full-back
	South Africa		
102	Mauro Bergamasco	1998–	Flanker
	Italy		
102	Dan Carter	2003–	Fly-half
	New Zealand		
101	David Campese	1982–96	Wing
	Australia		
101	Alessandro Troncon	1994–2007	Scrum-half
	Italy		
100	Adam Jones	2002–	Prop
	Wales (95), British and Irish Lions (5)		

100	Mils Muliaina New Zealand	2003–11	Full-back
100	Vasco Uva Portugal	2003–	Flanker
98	Raphaël Ibañez France	1996–2007	Hooker
98	Mike Phillips Wales (93), British and Irish Lions (5)	2003–	Scrum-half
98	Donncha O'Callaghan Ireland (94), British and Irish Lions (4)	2003–	Lock
98	Peter Stringer Ireland	2000–11	Scrum-half
97	Jonny Wilkinson England (91), British and Irish Lions (6)	1998–2011	Fly-half
96	Colin Charvis Wales (94), British and Irish Lions (2)	1996–2007	Flanker
95	Alun Wyn Jones Wales (89), British and Irish Lions (6)	2006–	Lock
94	Ma'a Nonu New Zealand	2003–	Centre
93	Serge Blanco France	1980–91	Full-back
93	Sean Lamont Scotland	2004–	Wing

92	Sean Fitzpatrick New Zealand	1986–97	Hooker
92	Matt Giteau Australia	2002–11	Fly-half
92	Martin Johnson England (84), British and Irish Lions (8)	1993–2003	Lock
92	Gareth Llewellyn Wales	1989–2005	Lock
92	Stephen Moore Australia	2005–	Hooker
92	Malcolm O'Kelly Ireland	1997–2009	Lock
92	Cristian Petre Romania	2001–12	Lock

MOST APPEARANCES FOR THE BRITISH AND IRISH LIONS

Willie John McBride (70)

Mike Gibson (68)

Syd Millar (44)

Delme Thomas (44)

Mike Campbell-Lamerton (42)

Andy Irvine (42)

Dickie Jeeps (42)

Gordon Brown (41)

Jack Jones (41)

Bryn Meredith (41)

MOST CAPPED IRISH INTERNATIONALS

Brian O'Driscoll (133)

Ronan O'Gara (128)

John Hayes (105)

Paul O'Connell (101)

Peter Stringer (98)

Donncha O'Callaghan (94)

Malcolm O'Kelly (92)

Rory Best (83)

Girvan Dempsey (82)

Gordon D'Arcy (81)

EUROPEAN (ERC) RUGBY PLAYER OF THE YEAR

2015	Nick Abendanon (Clermont Auvergne)
2014	Steffon Armitage (Toulon)
2013	Jonny Wilkinson (Toulon)
2012	Rob Kearney (Leinster)
2011	Sean O'Brien (Leinster)
2010	Ronan O'Gara (Munster)

IRB WORLD RUGBY PLAYER OF THE YEAR

2014   Brodie Retallick (New Zealand)

2013   Kieran Read (New Zealand)

2012   Dan Carter (New Zealand)

2011   Thierry Dusautoir (France)

2010   Richie McCaw (New Zealand)

2009   Richie McCaw (New Zealand)

2008   Shane Williams (Wales)

2007   Bryan Habana (South Africa)

2006   Richie McCaw (New Zealand)

2005   Dan Carter (New Zealand)

2004   Schalk Burger (South Africa)

2003   Jonny Wilkinson (England)

2002   Fabien Galthié (France)

2001   Keith Wood (Ireland)

IRUPA PLAYERS' PLAYER OF THE YEAR

2015   Paul O'Connell (Munster)

2014   Andrew Trimble (Ulster)

2013   Nick Williams (Ulster)

2012   Rob Kearney (Leinster)

2011   Isa Nacewa (Leinster)

2010   Tommy Bowe* (Ospreys)

2009   Brian O'Driscoll (Leinster)

2008   Tommy Bowe (Ospreys)

2007   Gordon D'Arcy (Leinster)

2006	Paul O'Connell (Munster)
2005	Johnny O'Connor (London Wasps)
2004	Gordon D'Arcy (Leinster)
2003	Malcolm O'Kelly (Leinster)

*Also Welsh Player of the Year

WORLD RUGBY HALL OF FAME

2014 inductees

Fred Allen (New Zealand)

Nathalie Amiel (France)

Bill Beaumont (England)

Gill Burns (England)

Don Clarke (New Zealand)

Ieuan Evans (Wales)

Sean Fitzpatrick (New Zealand)

Grant Fox (New Zealand)

Jim Greenwood (Scotland)

Carol Isherwood (England)

Patty Jervey (USA)

Michael Jones (New Zealand)

Ian Kirkpatrick (New Zealand)

John Kirwan (New Zealand)

Jason Leonard (England)

Michael Lynagh (Australia)

Jo Maso (France)

Terry McLean (New Zealand)

Colin Meads (New Zealand)

Graham Mourie (New Zealand)

George Nēpia (New Zealand)

Farah Palmer (New Zealand)

Anna Richards (New Zealand)

Keith Rowlands (Wales)

J. P. R. Williams (Wales)

Keith Wood (Ireland)

2013 inductees

David Bedell-Sivright (Scotland)

David Campese (Australia)

Ken Catchpole (Australia)

Ronnie Dawson (Ireland)

Mark Ella (Australia)

George Gregan (Australia)

Gavin Hastings (Scotland)

Thomas Lawton Snr (Australia)

Jack Matthews (Wales)

Robert Seddon and the 1888 British Lions (UK)

John Thornett (Australia)

Bleddyn Williams (Wales)

2012 inductees

1920 USA Olympic rugby team (USA)

1924 Romania Olympic rugby team (Romania)

1924 USA Olympic rugby team (USA)

Donald Campbell (Chile)

Ian Campbell (Chile)

Alfred St George Hamersley (England)

Vladimir Ilyushin (Soviet Union)

Yoshihiro Sakata (Japan)

Waisale Serevi (Fiji)

Gordon Tietjens (New Zealand)

Kennedy Tsimba (Zimbabwe)

Richard Tsimba (Zimbabwe)

2011 inductees

Kitch Christie (South Africa)

Bob Dwyer (Australia)

Nick Farr-Jones (Australia)

Martin Johnson (England)

John Kendall-Carpenter (England)

David Kirk (New Zealand)

Brian Lima (Samoa)

Richard Littlejohn (New Zealand)

Brian Lochore (New Zealand)

Jonah Lomu (New Zealand)

Rod Macqueen (Australia)

Francois Pienaar (South Africa)

Agustín Pichot (Argentina)

Gareth Rees (Canada)

Nicholas Shehadie (Australia)

John Smit (South Africa)

Roger Vanderfield (Australia)

Jake White (South Africa)

Clive Woodward (England)

2010 inductees

Barbarian Football Club (England)

Serge Blanco (France)

André Boniface (France)

Guy Boniface (France)

Cardiff Rugby Football Club (Wales)

William Percy Carpmael (England)

Dave Gallaher (New Zealand)

Mike Gibson (Ireland)

Frank Hancock (Wales)

Lucien Mias (France)

Jean Prat (France)

Alan Rotherham (England)

Harry Vassall (England)

2009 inductees

Barry Heatlie (South Africa)

Bill Maclagan (Scotland)

Willie John McBride (Ireland)

Ian McGeechan (Scotland)

Syd Millar (Ireland)

Cliff Morgan (Wales)

Tony O'Reilly (Ireland)

Bennie Osler (South Africa)

Frik du Preez (South Africa)

2008 inductees

1888–89 New Zealand Native football team (New Zealand)

Ned Haig (Scotland)

Jack Kyle (Ireland)

Melrose Rugby Football Club (Scotland)

Hugo Porta (Argentina)

Philippe Sella (France)

Joe Warbrick (New Zealand)

2007 inductees

Danie Craven (South Africa)

Pierre de Coubertin (France)

John Eales (Australia)

Gareth Edwards (Wales)

Wilson Whineray (New Zealand)

2006 inductees

William Webb Ellis (England)

Rugby School (England)

WIT AND WISDOM OF RUGBY

'Tony Ward is the most important rugby player in Ireland. His legs are far more important to his country than even those of Marlene Dietrich were to the film industry. A little hairier, maybe, but a pair of absolute winners.'

Mike Gibson, Irish rugby great, on the difference a great pair of legs can make.

'Knowledge is knowing a tomato is a fruit; wisdom is knowing not to put it in a fruit salad.'

Brian O'Driscoll explains the difference between a fruit and a fruit salad, while sounding suspiciously like a fruitcake!

'Bastareaud is like a black John Hayes that can move!'

Ronan O'Gara on his Ireland and Munster teammate, Speedy Gonzales Hayes.

'Shane Horgan could not be more right if he had come down from the mountain holding two tablets of stone.'

George Hook endorses the sentiments of fellow TV analyst, Leinster record try scorer and prophet Shane 'Moses' Horgan.

'You've got to get your first tackle in early, even if it's late.'

Welsh rugby centre Ray Gravell on the perfect tackle!

'I may not have been very tall or very athletic, but the one thing I did have was the most effective backside in world rugby.'

Former Irish international Jim Glennon suggests his game may not have been a thing of beauty.

'Me? As England's answer to Jonah Lomu? Joanna Lumley, more likely.'

England's Jonah Lomu impressionist, Damian Hopley, baring his soul.

'Don't ask me about emotions in the Welsh dressing room. I'm someone who cries when he watches Little House on the Prairie.'

Bob Norster, Welsh hard man, on the emotional inhabitants of Walnut Grove, aka the Welsh rugby team.

'The winger resembles Mother Brown, running with a high knee-lift and sometimes not progressing far from the spot where he started.'

Mark Reason from Total Sport *on the non-flying Irish winger, Simon Geoghegan.*

'Sometimes you have to put your balls on the line.'

Lions coach Warren Gatland digs deep to describe his decision to drop Brian O'Driscoll from the final Lions Test with Australia in July 2013.

'Look what these bastards have done to Wales. They've taken our coal, our water, our steel. They buy our houses and they only live in them for a fortnight every twelve months. What have they given us? Absolutely nothing. We've been exploited, raped, controlled and punished by the English, and that's who you are playing this afternoon.'

Phil Bennett giving another unemotional Welsh pre-game team talk before facing England.

'Prime Irish beef.'

Bill McLaren describing Irish legend Moss 'fillet steak' Keane.

'Rugby is a wonderful show: dance, opera and, suddenly, the blood of a killing.'

The actor Richard Burton revealing what most of us suspected already: that rugby is more than a simple matter of life and death.

'And it's a try by Hika the hooker from Ngongotaha.'

Commentator Bill McLaren was never one to mince his words.

'Every time I went to tackle him, Horrocks went one way, Taylor went the other, and all I got was the bloody hyphen.'

Trying to tackle Phil Horrocks-Taylor really did spell trouble for Nick England.

'Mothers keep their photo on the mantelpiece to stop the kids going too near the fire.'

Jim Neilly (on BBC TV in 1995) reveals that the Munster pack did not just put the fear of God into the opposition!

'Remember that rugby is a team game; all 14 of you make sure you pass the ball to Jonah Lomu.'

A fax to the All Blacks before the 1995 World Cup semi-final dispels the myth that the All Blacks were a one-man team!

'Rugby is great. The players don't wear helmets or padding; they just beat the living daylights out of each other and then go for a beer. I love that.'

Joe Theismann, former American football great, and fan of blood sports!

'The relationship between the Welsh and the English is based on trust and understanding. They don't trust us and we don't understand them.'

Dudley Wood, English RFU secretary, on English and Welsh rugby values.

'I wouldn't say he played on the wing: he was on the wing would be more accurate. The conditions did not suit him.'

The great Willie John McBride commenting on Tony O'Reilly's final non-performance for his country against England.

'Johnny O'Connor is a guy who puts his head where a blacksmith wouldn't put an anvil.'

George Hook on the hard-headed former Connacht and Irish international flanker.

'You can add Thomond Park to Fatima, Knock and Lourdes. The lame will come here and walk. They'll be selling water here, because this defies logic.'

George Hook after Munster had performed rugby's version of the great escape against Gloucester.

'You're not a rugby player unless you've been dropped!'

Ireland's finest, Jack Kyle, on the importance of 'bench service'.

'For crying out loud, you're putting Shergar where you wouldn't put Royal Tan over the fences at Aintree. Give him some space to play in.'

George Hook on horsing around with Brian O'Driscoll at inside centre.

'Everybody thinks we should have moustaches and hairy arses, but in fact you could put us all on the cover of *Vogue*.'

Helen Kirk on why rugby truly is the beautiful game.

'His sidestep was marvellous – like a shaft of lightning.'

Bill McLaren on the man who proved lightning strikes more than twice, Welsh wizard Gerald Davies.

'This would be the greatest achievement ever,' rugby pundit George Hook tells Tom McGurk ahead of the Grand Slam decider between Ireland and England.

'Why?' McGurk replies.

'Because when our lads defeated the English to win it in 1947 [*sic*] at Ravenhill, the opposition had been at war for six years and were unprepared and undernourished. We, on the other hand had been in intensive training and were filled with rashers and sausages. It was a mismatch.'

Like Napoleon, George Hook believes an army marches on its stomach!

'There is far too much talk about good ball and bad ball. In my opinion, good ball is when you have possession and bad ball is when the opposition have it.'

Dick Jeeps on why any ball is better than no ball.

'He's like Bambi on speed.'

Bill McLaren on Mother Brown, aka Simon Geoghegan.

'I'd like to thank the press from the heart of my bottom.'

England's Nick Easter thanks the press from the bottom of his bottom after they had silenced the doubters with their World Cup quarter-final win over Australia.

After biting Sean Fitzpatrick's ear: 'For an eighteen-month suspension, I feel I probably should have torn it off. Then at least I could say, "Look, I've returned to South Africa with the guy's ear."'

The Boks' Johan le Roux on rugby and big game hunting.

'They say down at Stradey that if ever you catch him [Phil Bennett] you get to make a wish.'

Bill McLaren again, on the need to be careful what you wish for.

On his successors in the Oxford University backs: 'I've seen better centres in a box of Black Magic.'

Rugby life is like a box of chocolates for former Oxford University back Joe 'Forrest Gump' McPartlin.

On playing for Wales at Lansdowne Road: 'I didn't know what was going on at the start in the swirling wind. The flags were all pointing in different directions and I thought the Irish had starched them just to fool us.'

Mike Watkins knows the meaning of an ill wind in Dublin.

'I think you enjoy the game more if you don't know the rules. Anyway, you're on the same wavelength as the referees.'

Jonathan Davies speaking on A Question of Sport about questionable refereeing.

'No leadership, no ideas. Not even enough imagination to thump someone in the line-up when the ref wasn't looking.'

J. P. R. Williams bemoans the lack of imagination in the Welsh play as they succumbed 28–9 to the Wallabies.

After John Jeffrey had dropped and badly damaged the Calcutta Cup: 'It will now have to be called the Calcutta Shield.'

Bob Munro on the birth of a new trophy for the annual England v Scotland encounter.

'The only hope for the England rugby union team is to play it all for laughs. It would pack them in if the public address system at Twickenham was turned up full blast to record the laughs at every inept bit of passing, kicking or tackling. The nation would be in fits ... and on telly the BBC would not need a commentator but just a tape of that Laughing Policeman, turning it loud at the most hilarious bits.'

Jim Rivers in a letter to The Guardian *in 1979, on the most entertaining English rugby team of all time.*

'I don't know about us not having a Plan B when things went wrong; we looked like we didn't have a Plan A.'

Geoff Cooke on England's best-laid plans after they had been humbled by New Zealand in the 1995 World Cup semi-final.

'Most Misleading Campaign of 1991: England's Rugby World Cup squad, who promoted a scheme called "Run with the Ball". Not, unfortunately, among themselves.'

Time Out *magazine on the hazards of self-promotion.*

After J. P. R. Williams was involved in a road traffic accident: 'Bloody typical, isn't it? The car's a write-off. The tanker's a write-off. But J. P. R. comes out of it all in one piece.'

Gareth Edwards of Wales on hearing that his team-mate is as elusive off the pitch as on it.

'It's the first time I've been cold for seven years.'

Welsh rugby great Jonathan Davies on the hazards of switching codes from rugby league back to rugby union.

'We've lost seven of our last eight matches. Only team that we've beaten was Western Samoa. Good job we didn't play the whole of Samoa.'

When rugby tours go bad, by Gareth Davies.

'I never comment on referees and I'm not going to break the habit of a lifetime for that prat.'

Ewan McKenzie declines to comment on the referee's performance, or lack of it.

Following Scotland's accusations of French foul play: 'If you can't take a punch, you should play table tennis.'

Pierre Berbizier of France alludes to what most of us knew already – real men play table tennis.

'A forward's usefulness to his side varies as to the square of his distance from the ball.'

Clarrie Gibbons puts forward the theory that forwards are not very useful.

'Rugby backs can be identified because they generally have clean jerseys and identifiable partings in their hair … come the revolution the backs will be the first to be lined up against the wall and shot for living parasitically off the work of others.'

Peter FitzSimons hints that when the going gets tough, the rugby backs get going – in the opposite direction!

'In 1823 William Webb Ellis first picked up the ball in his arms and ran with it. And for the next 156 years forwards have been trying to work out why.'

A rather accurate description by Sir Tasker Watkins, of the Human Shield, otherwise known as the rugby forward.

'Rugby is a game for the mentally deficient … That is why it was invented by the British. Who else but an Englishman could invent an oval ball?'

Peter Pook on why England has the patent on oddballs.

'As you run around Battersea Park in them, looking like a cross between a member of the SAS and Blake's 7, there is always the lingering fear of arrest.'

Brian Moore on the perils of wearing England's new rubber training suit.

'The pub is as much a part of rugby as is the playing field.'

John Dickinson on the spiritual home of rugby.

'That was the latest tackle I've ever seen!'

An enraged referee berating Lions centre Ray Gravell for a tackle against The Orange Free State.

'Sorry, ref, I got there as quickly as I could.'

Gravell issuing an apology of sorts.

'I told him, "Son, what is it with you? Is it ignorance or apathy?" He said, "David, I don't know and I don't care."'

When asked by David Nucifora of Auckland about his attitude to the game, Troy Flavell keeps it short, sweet and sharp.

'Strangely, in slow-motion replay, the ball seemed to hang in the air for even longer.'

Commentator Murray Mexted, never a man to state the obvious.

'I would not say he [Rico Gear] is the best left winger in the Super 14, but there are none better.'

Murray Mexted still refusing to state the obvious!

'That kick was absolutely unique, except for the one before it, which was identical.'

Tony Brown of New Zealand making the extraordinary look ordinary.

COMMENTATORS AND
TV ANALYSTS

GEORGE HOOK

– George Hook was born on 19 May 1941.

– He had a career as a rugby union coach and businessman, before becoming a rugby pundit with Raidió Teilifís Éireann.

– *The Right Hook*, Hook's radio show on Newstalk, is a popular drive-time programme.

– George and fellow RTÉ analyst Brent Pope chaired the *Heineken Cup Roadshow* on RTÉ 2. The popular duo presented the show from various locations around Ireland.

– Hook grew up in Cork and attended Presentation Brothers College. He later attended Rathmines College of Commerce.

– He coached London Irish and Connacht. He also coached the United States Eagles and in 1987 led them to the first-ever World Cup, in New Zealand.

– In 2005 he published an autobiography, *Time Added On*. The book described his business career and its failure. His second book is called *This is Rugby*.

- He has appeared as a judge on the RTÉ dancing show *Celebrity Jigs 'n' Reels*.

- George Hook is also president of The Lord's Taverners Ireland, a charity for disabled young people and those with special needs.

BRENT POPE

- Brent Pope was born in New Zealand in 1961.

- In his early career he played as a forward for various teams, including Mid Canterbury, Canterbury, Lincoln University and Otago.

- Pope spent almost ten years at Otago and played nearly 100 first-class games with the team. During that time he formed potent partnerships with the likes of All Blacks Paul Henderson, Mike Brewer, Taine Randall, Josh Kronfeld, Arane Pene and Jamie Joseph.

- His dreams of playing for New Zealand in the 1987 World Cup were quashed when he had to withdraw a week before the tournament began due to a serious elbow injury picked up in the final series of All Black trials.

- Pope returned to form after the injury and was nominated as one of New Zealand's outstanding domestic players of that year.

- Pope was named Otago player of the year in 1988. He was shortlisted for the All Blacks tour to

Japan at the end of that year, but missed the final cut when the squad was trimmed to twenty-four players.

– He came to Ireland in 1991, to play for St Mary's RFC. He then coached both St Mary's and Clontarf to three separate national division All Ireland League titles, three Floodlit Cups and two Leinster Senior Cups (the first Clontarf had won since 1956).

– Pope led St Mary's to victory in the 2000 AIB League Division 1, the first Leinster-based coach to do so.

– He has been one of RTÉ's main rugby pundits since 1993.

– In 2012 he released a bestselling autobiography entitled *Brent Pope: If You Really Knew Me* and has also written a series of children's books including *Woody: A Whale of a Tale.*

BILL McLAREN

– Bill McLaren, known as the voice of rugby, was born in Hawick, in the Scottish Borders, in 1923.

– McLaren was a useful flank forward and played for Hawick RFC before the Second World War.

– He served with the Royal Artillery in Italy during the war. He was used as a forward spotter and

- on one occasion was confronted by a mound of 1,500 corpses in an Italian cemetery.

- He was selected for a Scotland trial in 1947 and was widely tipped to be given a full international call-up, but contracted tuberculosis, which ended his playing career.

- McLaren made his national debut for BBC Radio in 1953. His native Scotland lost the game 12–0 to Wales.

- His first television commentary came six years later. He was one of many post-war commentators who progressed from commentating on BBC Radio to BBC Television.

- In November 2001 he became the first non-rugby international to be inducted into the International Rugby Hall of Fame.

- He was awarded an MBE in 1992, an OBE in 1995 and a CBE in 2003.

- McLaren featured as a commentator on the video games *Jonah Lomu Rugby* and *EA Rugby 2001*.

- His final commentary was for a Wales v Scotland match in 2002. The crowd sang 'For He's a Jolly Good Fellow' and a Welsh supporter displayed a banner stating 'Bill McLaren is Welsh'.

- After retirement, McLaren wrote the book *Rugby's Great Heroes and Entertainers* in 2003. He died in January 2010 at the age of eighty-six.

THE WEIRD AND WONDERFUL WORLD OF RUGBY

- The same whistle is used to kick off the opening game of every Rugby World Cup tournament. It is the Gil Evans whistle and was first blown by Gil Evans, a Welsh referee, in a match between England and New Zealand in 1905. The iconic whistle was also used at the kick-off of the final rugby match at the 1924 Paris Olympics.

- All Black Cyril Brownie was the first player ever to be red-carded, in a game in 1925 against England.

- If the teams that reached the last four of the 2011 Rugby World Cup were feeling a sense of déjà vu, they could be forgiven. The same countries contested the 1987 World Cup semi-finals. The same two teams then reached the final (France and New Zealand), meaning there was exactly the same third-place play-off (Wales v Australia) as in 1987. The finalists, France and New Zealand, would face off in Eden Park, where the 1987 decider had been held!

- Ever wonder why rugby balls are oval? The first-ever rugby balls were fashioned out of hand-stitched leather casings and pigs' bladders. Apparently pigs' bladders naturally take on an oval shape.

- As rugby balls and footballs were made from pigs' bladders and they had to be blown up by breath alone, you could become ill if you blew up a diseased bladder. The wife of Richard Lindon, a man who made balls for Rugby School in the nineteenth century, died after breathing in the air from too many bad bladders.

- Jonny Wilkinson missed his first three drop-goal attempts in the 2003 Rugby World Cup final. He avoided missing four in a row by slotting the match-winning score at the fourth attempt!

- The Six Nations has a number of trophies apart from the Calcutta Cup. Since 1988 the Millennium Trophy has been awarded to the winners of the fixture between England and Ireland. From 1989 the Centenary Quaich has been awarded to the winners of the game contested by Ireland and Scotland. Since 2007 France and Italy have contested the Giuseppe Garibaldi Trophy. It was created to mark the two-hundredth anniversary of the birth of Giuseppe Garibaldi.

- Leinster and Munster are two of rugby's greatest rivals. They have played out many high-scoring encounters, including Munster's 45–40 win in 1997. Back in 1954 the two Irish provinces played out the lowest scoring match, a 0–0 draw!

- The longest recorded successful drop goal is 77.7 metres (85 yards), by Gerry Hamilton Brand on 2

January 1932 for South Africa, against England, at Twickenham.

– The fastest try in a rugby union match was scored after just 7.24 seconds by Tyson Lewis for Doncaster Knights Club, against Old Albanians, at St Albans, on 23 November 2013. The try was scored direct from kick-off as the winger raced onto the ball that had bounced over the head of an Old Albanians player.

– Thomas Gisborne Gordon, who was an Irish international between 1877–78, holds a very special record. He is the only one-handed player to have competed in international rugby in either code.

– The oldest person to win a double cap in international rugby, by playing in both codes, is Thomas Calnan. Aged thirty-six years and fifty days, he made his debut for the UAE rugby union side against Hong Kong in Dubai on 11 December 2012. On 30 March 2012 he represented the UAE rugby league side in a match against Pakistan. Both matches are fully recognised international Test matches.

– The most siblings to play in a rugby union international match is five. Archie, Jack, Frank, George and Max Skofic all lined out for Slovenia against Bulgaria in a European Nations Cup Second Division match at Park Siska, Ljubljana, Slovenia, on 12 April 2014. Archie, George and

Frank started the game and played the entire 80 minutes. Max entered the fray after 25 minutes and scored a hat-trick of tries. George also scored a try, while Frank kicked a conversion. Jack was introduced after 77 minutes. All five brothers capped a great day by finishing on the winning side, as Slovenia defeated Bulgaria 43–17.

- Ireland turned up two men short for their game in Cardiff in 1884 and had to borrow two Welsh players.

- The longest game in history took place on 1 June 2013 and lasted for 24 hours and 51 minutes. It took place at the Leicester Tigers' stadium between a team representing the charity Scotty's Little Soldiers and an Armed Forces XV.

- The biggest lead in the history of international rugby union was taken by Argentina over Paraguay in May 2002. They won 152–0.

- In 1981 Irish rugby legend Tony Ward played for Limerick United in the UEFA Cup, and in 1982 he helped them win the FAI Cup. Ward, who starred for Munster in their historic win over the All Blacks, also played for fierce interprovincial rivals Leinster.

- The USA are still the reigning Olympic rugby champions. This is because they were the last team to win, in 1924. The sport has not been played at the Olympic Games since.

- Tries are unique to the game of rugby. The try is so called because originally players didn't receive any points for crossing the line. Instead the reward was an opportunity to try a kick at goal.

- In international rugby, the player who has scored the highest number of tries is Daisuke Ohata of Japan. He has scored sixty-nine tries in fifty-eight matches.

- There are a number of clubs that claim to be the oldest rugby club in the world, including Barnes RFC, which claims to have been founded in 1839, Guy's Hospital, founded in 1843, and Dublin University Football Club, founded in 1854.

- Welsh rugby legend Gareth Edwards was no stranger to setting records on and off the pitch. A keen angler, he set a British angling record in 1990 when he landed a pike weighing 45lb 6oz at Llandegfedd Reservoir, near Pontypool. Edwards held the record for two years.

- Rugby is the national sport of seven countries: Fiji, Georgia, Madagascar, New Zealand, Samoa, Tonga and Wales.

- Unlike in cricket, where both countries must grant Test status for a match to be considered a Test, rugby union requires only one nation to recognise a match as a Test in order for it to be included in Test statistics for that nation.

- The British and Irish Lions and Pacific Islanders

do not represent a single nation but are also considered Test teams because they are selected by a group of recognised national unions.

- The oldest international rugby union player is Mark Spencer, who was born on 21 May 1954. He was aged fifty-seven years and 340 days when he represented Qatar in the Asian Five Nations against Uzbekistan, in Dubai on 25 April 2012.

- The previous record holder was the legendary Hugo Porta of Argentina. He played at the age of forty-seven years and 218 days in 1999, against a World XV.

- The Super 15 rugby trophy was designed by leading Sydney-based consultancy Blue Sky, and manufactured by Box and Dice, a specialised prototype and production company. The two companies have worked on a number of award-winning design projects, amongst them the Sydney 2000 Olympic Torch.

- The Wooden Spoon is the rather dubious prize for finishing last in the Six Nations. Since the beginning of the competition in 2000, only Ireland and England have managed to avoid the dreaded kitchen utensil.

- The old Six Nations trophy has a capacity of 3.75 litres. The good news for the more celebratory types is that this is sufficient for five bottles of champagne. Within the mahogany base is a concealed drawer that contains six emblems, one for each of the competing nations, which can be screwed onto the detachable lid.

- Eden Park, host to two Rugby World Cup finals, was originally a swamp.

- The record number of wins in the Women's Rugby World Cup is three, by Farah Palmer of New Zealand. She played for the Black Ferns in the 1998, 2002 and 2006 tournaments.

REELING IN THE RUGBY YEARS

- The emergence of rugby football is commonly attributed to an incident during a game of English school football at Rugby School in 1823. William Webb Ellis is said to have picked up the ball and run with it. This story has never been authenticated and its origin is thought to lie more in romance than reason. What is certain, however, is that the game was first played at the school and that former pupils then introduced it to their universities.

- The first rules of the game were drawn up at Rugby School in 1845. They were then followed by the Cambridge Rules in 1848.

- Blackheath was the first club formed as a soccer club to take up rugby. In 1863 the club left the Football Association. This break from soccer was the first clear signal that rugby would be a separate entity.

- The Rugby Football Union was formed in 1871. The game was originally called rugby football, but a split within the group led to one side being called rugby union and the other rugby league. The two separate codes were born in 1875.

- Albert Pell, who was a student at Cambridge, is credited with the formation of the first rugby team.

- The first-ever international match took place on 27 March 1871 between England and Scotland. Scotland won the match by two tries and one penalty goal to a single England try. The match was played in Raeburn, Edinburgh, in front of 4,000 spectators.

- By 1881 both Ireland and Wales had their own teams, leading to the inauguration of the first international competition, the Home Nations Championship, in 1883.

- The Melrose Sevens tournament was first run in 1883 as seven-a-side rugby was gaining in popularity. The tournament is still in existence today.

- 1888 brought another milestone as a British Isles selection toured Australia and New Zealand. The tour was a private venture but it proved to be the forerunner to the British and Irish Lions tours. In the same season a New Zealand Native football team brought the first overseas team to British shores.

- From 1905 to 1908 all three major southern-hemisphere rugby countries sent touring teams to the northern hemisphere: New Zealand (The Originals) toured in 1905, followed by South Africa in 1906 and Australia in 1908. All three teams brought innovative styles of play and demonstrated superior fitness levels. The tourists also placed greater emphasis on tactics.

- In 1905 the New Zealand touring team performed a haka, the first time the traditional Maori dance had been seen on these shores. Teddy Morgan of Wales then led the crowd in singing the Welsh national anthem, the first singing of a national anthem at a sporting fixture.

- In 1905 France played their first-ever international fixture, against England.

- The Five Nations Championship began in 1910.

- Rugby union was played at four Olympic Games during the early twentieth century.

- No international rugby matches took place during the First World War. There were a number of service matches between army teams. The annual varsity match between Cambridge and Oxford was one of the few fixtures that continued to be played.

- The Scottish Rugby Union centenary celebrations included the first officially sanctioned international sevens tournament. It took place at Murrayfield in 1973.

- The first women's rugby international was staged on 13 June 1982 as part of the Dutch Rugby Union's fiftieth anniversary. France defeated Holland 4–0 in Utrecht.

- In 1987 the first Rugby World Cup was staged, which the All Blacks won.

- In 1991 the first Women's Rugby World Cup was staged in Wales. The USA emerged as winners, defeating England 19–6.

- 1993 saw another World Cup first when the World Cup Sevens tournament was held at Murrayfield. Sevens rugby has been added to the 2016 Olympic Games.

- Rugby union became a professional sport in 1995. The IRB declared the game open in 1995, paving the way for player payment.

- The introduction of professionalism spawned a host of new club competitions, including the Heineken Cup in the northern hemisphere and Super Rugby in the southern hemisphere.

- The Tri Nations, an annual tournament involving the Australian, New Zealand and South African teams, kicked off in 1996.

- The first-ever Heineken Cup final was staged at Cardiff Arms Park in 1996. Toulouse defeated Cardiff 21–18.

- Scotland won the last ever Five Nations Championship, in 1999. The RBS Six Nations began at the dawn of a new millennium, with the original five nations and a new addition, Italy.

- The World Rugby Player of the Year award was introduced in 2001. Keith Wood of Ireland was the first-ever winner.

- In 2012 the Tri Nations was expanded to include Argentina. The newcomers had risen impressively in the world rankings, including finishing in a lofty third position in the 2007 Rugby World Cup.

- Rugby Union is now played in over 100 countries and on six continents. In 2014 there were 101 nations affiliated to the IRB, and there were also eighteen associate members.

BIBLIOGRAPHY

Books

Bond, K., Clark, R., and Griffiths, J., *World Rugby Yearbook 2015* (Vision Sports Publishing, Surrey, 2014)

Jones, C., *The Secret Life of Twickenham* (Aurum Press, London, 2014)

McCaw, R., *The Real McCaw* (Aurum Press, London, 2013)

O'Gara, R., *Ronan O'Gara: My Autobiography* (Transworld Ireland, Dublin, 2009)

Wilkinson, J., *Jonny: My Autobiography* (Headline, London, 2012)

Websites

www.allgreatquotes.com
www.connachtrugby.ie
www.epcrugby.com
www.espn.co.uk/rugby/
www.espnscrum.com
www.guinnessworldrecords.com
intheloose.com
www.irishrugby.ie
www.leinsterrugby.ie
www.lionsrugby.com
www.munsterrugby.ie
www.planetrugby.com
www.pro12rugby.com
www.rfu.com
www.scorepro.com
www.ulsterrugby.ie
www.wikipedia.org
www.worldrugby.org